Jump Start Sketch

by Daniel Schwarz

Copyright © 2016 SitePoint Pty. Ltd.

Product Manager: Simon Mackie   **Technical Editor:** Darin Dimitrov
English Editor: Ralph Mason   **Cover Designer:** Alex Walker

Notice of Rights

Notice of Liability

The author and publisher have made every effort to ensure the accuracy of the information herein. However, the information contained in this book is sold without warranty, either express or implied. Neither the authors and SitePoint Pty. Ltd., nor its dealers or distributors will be held liable for any damages to be caused either directly or indirectly by the instructions contained in this book, or by the software or hardware products described herein.

Trademark Notice

Rather than indicating every occurrence of a trademarked name as such, this book uses the names only in an editorial fashion and to the benefit of the trademark owner with no intention of infringement of the trademark.

Published by SitePoint Pty. Ltd.

48 Cambridge Street Collingwood
VIC Australia 3066
Web: www.sitepoint.com
Email: books@sitepoint.com

ISBN 978-0-9943469-6-4 (print)

ISBN 978-0-9943470-2-2 (ebook)
Printed and bound in the United States of America

About Daniel Schwarz

Daniel[1] is a designer, writer, and now author. He's also a digital nomad, travelling the world with his beloved wife and earning his bucks writing about various design-related topics, and his *other* beloved: Sketch. He founded Airwalk Studios[2], which is working on books and magazines for designers and digital nomads. He and his wife both run the company from Airbnb's and local cafés.

About SitePoint

SitePoint specializes in publishing fun, practical, and easy-to-understand content for web professionals. Visit http://www.sitepoint.com/ to access our blogs, books, newsletters, articles, and community forums. You'll find a stack of information on JavaScript, PHP, Ruby, mobile development, design, and more.

[1.] https://mrdaniels.ch
[2.] http://airwalk-studios.com

Table of Contents

Chapter 2   **Artboards, Layers, and Styling**

Chapter 3   Shared Styles and Symbols.............37

Chapter 4   Smart Guides and Snapping 56

Chapter 5   Vector and Bitmap Editing Tools .68

Appendix A **Keyboard Shortcuts and Useful Resources** 135

Preface

Sketch is a vector-based design app that has become a well-established tool for interface designers, mainly due to its ability to export assets in a variety of resolutions.

It takes web and app design to a new level, thanks to its minimalist approach to software design and intuitive features such as Smart Guides, Shared Styles and the ability to export layers on a whim.

Sketch offers features that are particularly important to user interface designers: an improved method of aligning layers or even entire components; the ability to export layers in a variety of resolutions; the functionality to save styles that can be reused time and time again; and, perhaps most importantly, ways to accomplish these things without having to dig through menus or to use complex keyboard shortcuts.

Not only has Photoshop started to adopt some of Sketch's most useful concepts, but Sketch has begun to return the favor. An intense rivalry is forcing a huge shift in the way we design for screens—at a rate so accelerated that it's a particularly exciting time to be a user interface designer.

For the number crunchers out there, the Subtraction Design Tools Survey[1] explains that 34% of designers use Sketch for interface design, in comparison to the 29% that use Adobe Photoshop. It could be argued that Photoshop is only just behind Sketch because Photoshop (along with the other Adobe apps) is available for both Windows and Mac, while Sketch is only available to Mac OS X users.

[1.] http://tools.subtraction.com/interface-design.html

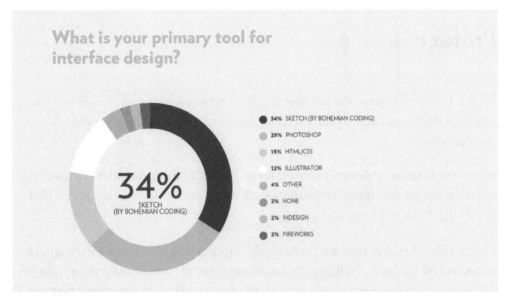

0-1. 34% of interface designers use Sketch

What Sketch Is

Sketch is a Mac app that's particularly popular for designing user interfaces. Being a vector-based tool, it's also well suited to icon and logo design. It plays a similar role to Adobe's Illustrator and Fireworks apps (the latter of which has now been abandoned by Adobe).

Bohemian Coding, the company behind Sketch, says it has no plans to make a Windows OS counterpart, because Sketch is built on native Mac OS code that allows extra functionality, such as version history. Not only does that also keep Sketch running smoothly, but it means Bohemian Coding can design Sketch to look and feel like a Mac app.

Why Sketch Gets Compared with Photoshop

From a practical point of view, comparing Sketch (a user interface design tool) with Photoshop (a *photo* manipulation tool) doesn't make sense. However, designers *do* compare them, because Photoshop has long been an industry standard for designers of all types. In the past, there was less of a focus on user interface design, and thus there weren't apps catering for it specifically.

Photoshop is the main tool that Sketch users have been switching *from*, so that's what Sketch tends to be compared with, even though Photoshop doesn't look or act much like Sketch. Being a vector-based app *not originally designed to manipulate photos*, Sketch is more akin to Fireworks and Illustrator than to Photoshop.

What Sketch Isn't

Sketch isn't a multi-functional (or over-functional) tool like Photoshop. Because of this, it has a much cleaner, more minimal user interface that makes designing with it a complete delight. Sketch was built for designing web and app components and nothing else—and its user interface reflects that.

The images below highlight the distinct difference between Sketch's interface and Photoshop's.

0-2. Sketch's minimal interface

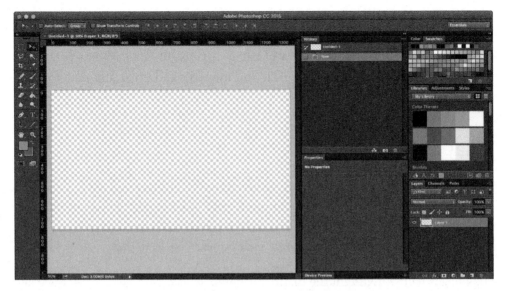

0-3. Photoshop's not-so-minimal interface

Photoshop has begun to implement some of Sketch's best features—such as **Artboards**, **Smart Guides** and the critically-acclaimed **Export** function (which Photoshop calls "Generate Assets"). However, Photoshop isn't (and never has been) specifically built for designing interfaces, and it still lacks much of what user interface designers need, while offering too much of what interface designers *don't* need. Sketch's relative simplicity also lends it greater speed and intuitiveness.

Quite intentionally, Sketch doesn't offer image editing functionality—even though it does have tools for simple blurring and color management. So it's definitely not a replacement for Photoshop in that respect.

Comparing Sketch, Photoshop, and Illustrator

No one tool can do everything, so it's useful to be clear on what each tool does best. Here's a simple guide to which tools to use for various tasks.

Sketch is best suited for:

- designing vector-based icons
- creating basic logos and logotypes

- designing web or app user interfaces
- working with basic SVGs (Scalable Vector Graphics)

Photoshop is best suited for:

- manipulating bitmap images
- making 3D or highly detailed imagery
- painting digital artworks

Illustrator is best suited for:

- illustrating digital artworks
- designing complex icons
- working with highly detailed typography
- graphic designing with vector requirements
- working with elaborate SVGs for the web
- designing *complex print* media

Trialing and Buying Sketch

You can snag a trial copy on Sketch's website[2]. Though originally available via the Mac App Store, Bohemian Coding now requires the app to be purchased directly from its site, as that ensures third-party integrations will work correctly. The only other requirement is that your Mac is running at least OS X 10.9, also known as **Mavericks**. When the trial runs out, Sketch is $129.

Who Should Read This Book

This book is for beginner to intermediate level web designers. You don't need any prior experience with Sketch, although some experience with another design tool, such as Photoshop, will be useful.

---

[2] https://www.sketchapp.com

Conventions Used

You'll notice that we've used certain typographic and layout styles throughout this book to signify different types of information. Look out for the following items.

Code Samples

Code in this book is displayed using a fixed-width font, like so:

```
<h1>A Perfect Summer's Day</h1>
 <p>It was a lovely day for a walk in the park. The
↳ birds were singing and the kids were all back at
↳ school.</p>
```

If the code is to be found in the book's code archive, the name of the file will appear at the top of the program listing, like this:

0-4. example.css

```
.footer {
  background-color: #CCC;
  border-top: 1px solid #333;
}
```

If only part of the file is displayed, this is indicated by the word *excerpt*:

0-5. example.css *(excerpt)*

```
.footer {
  background-color: #CCC;
  border-top: 1px solid #333;
}
```

If additional code is to be inserted into an existing example, the new code will be displayed in bold:

```
function animate() {
  new_variable = "Hello";
}
```

Where existing code is required for context, rather than repeat all of it, ⋮ will be displayed:

```
function animate() {
  ⋮
  new_variable = "Hello";
}
```

Some lines of code should be entered on one line, but we've had to wrap them because of page constraints. An ↪ indicates a line break that exists for formatting purposes only, and should be ignored:

```
URL.open("http://www.sitepoint.com/responsive-web-design-real
↪ -user-testing/?responsive1");
```

Tips, Notes, and Warnings

 ### Hey, You!

Tips provide helpful little pointers.

 ### Ahem, Excuse Me ...

Notes are useful asides that are related—but not critical—to the topic at hand. Think of them as extra tidbits of information.

Make Sure You Always ...

... pay attention to these important points.

Watch Out!

Warnings highlight any gotchas that are likely to trip you up along the way.

Supplementary Materials

- https://github.com/spbooks/jssketch1 has downloadable example files and a printable keyboard cheat sheet.
- https://www.sitepoint.com/community/ are SitePoint's forums, for help on any tricky web problems.
- **books@sitepoint.com** is our email address, should you need to contact us to report a problem, or for any other reason.

Chapter **1**

Sketch's Interface

It's often said that the best user interfaces are invisible, or "the best interface is no interface". A feature that simply works by itself—without requiring interaction with the interface—is the ideal approach to completing an action, while those that require several interactions are less than optimal.

Smart Guides is one such feature of Sketch that mostly works without having to interact further with the canvas, showing you the distance of a layer relative to another layer *while* you drag it across the canvas. There's *no interface* for that.

Sketch also has a concise list of easy-to-remember keyboard shortcuts like **R** for Rectangle, enabling the user interface to be quite small. While it may seem a little bare in comparison to apps like Photoshop and Illustrator, Sketch is *anything* but limited. You can open yourself to an extremely efficient workflow if you learn the keyboard shortcut equivalent to each interaction, although you won't find Sketch difficult if you work better with a mouse. Your only real limitation is your creativity.

At a Glance: Comparing Sketch to Adobe's Apps

Despite Adobe introducing a fresh, flat design skin to its user interfaces back in December 2015, these interfaces are still rather clunky in comparison to Sketch. Sketch has a Layer List, an Inspector and of course a toolbar, whereas Adobe apps have the option to add and remove tools from the workspace. Sketch has a single, default workspace that's easier for a learner to master.

Everything Sketch has to offer can be visible on the screen all at once: there's no need to optimize workspaces.

1-6. Sketch UI with all tabs visible

Canvases

Whenever you first open Sketch, you'll be staring at a blank **canvas**, which is essentially a white background that you can't interact with. It's a space for creating and nothing more.

As you may have noticed already, the blank canvas is unlimited; until you create an Artboard, there are no bounds. **Artboards** are a different type of space to work in; they have *predefined* dimensions and they're inserted *into* the canvas. We'll talk about Artboards in much more detail in the next chapter.

Layers are the individual components that make up a design (which can be a shape, some text or a vector of some sort). We'll discuss them extensively over the course of this book.

Pages are another concept in Sketch, where each Page houses another unlimited canvas. On each canvas you can have unlimited Artboards/screens, and the layers are created within them.

Pages → Canvas → Artboards → Layers.

Multiple Canvases

Sketch doesn't have tabbed windows. Any new documents (**cmd + N**) will appear in a new window—which may seem a little awkward, but it's actually commonplace to use Sketch's unlimited canvas for all screens related to a design. You can have as many Artboards and as many screens as you need in the canvas. In the unlikely case of layer overcrowding, you can split the document across multiple Pages, but you'll never require multiple windows. (We'll talk more about that shortly.)

Canvas Zooming

When using Sketch's unlimited canvas, you may end up with quite a few Artboards on the screen at once. Luckily, Sketch has multiple keyboard shortcuts for zooming in and out:

- Zoom in: **cmd + plus sign**
- Zoom out: **cmd + minus sign**
- Zoom to actual canvas size: **cmd + 0**
- Zoom to canvas center: **cmd + 1**
- Zoom into selected layer: **cmd + 2**
- Center selection on the screen: **cmd + 3**

Don't worry if you have trouble remembering these. I'll reiterate keyboard shortcuts throughout the book, and you can always flick to the end of the book to see a complete list of Sketch shortcuts.

Layer List

Layers and Groups (of layers) appear in a list on the left-hand side of the app's window. We call this the **Layer List**. It works no differently from Photoshop's layer list, only in Photoshop it appears on the right. If a layer appears at the top of the list, then it appears on top of any other layer in the canvas. We call this **layer hierarchy**.

You can drag layers in the list to reorder them, but it's easier to use the keyboard shortcuts. Simply hold **cmd + option** and move the arrow keys up/down to edit the hierarchy of a layer.

Shape Layers

Shapes are the most common type of layer. By shapes I mean rectangles, ovals, and the many other shapes you can insert, such as stars, triangles, rounded-corner rectangles and more. Here are some handy keyboard shortcuts:

- Oval: **O**
- Rectangle: **R**
- Rounded Rectangle: U
- Line: **L**

More shapes can be accessed via the menu bar with **Insert → Shape**, although you won't need those shapes very often. Once you've selected a shape, drag the mouse to draw it on the canvas. Getting the correct dimensions isn't a big deal, since we can style shapes and other types of layers very easily.

1-7. A simple rectangle ("Rectangle 1") as shown on both the canvas and in the Layer List

Text Layers

Similarly to shapes, text can be created by using the keyboard shortcut **T** and drawing out the layer. When you've finished typing out the text, you can use **esc** on the keyboard to snap out of editing mode and move the layer around once more.

1-8. A simple text layer ("hello") as shown on both the canvas and in the Layer List

Selecting and Hiding Layers

You can select a text layer by either clicking on it in the canvas or selecting it from the Layer List. You can hide the layer by hovering over it in the Layer List and clicking the "eye" icon that appears. Click it once more to reveal it again.

Reordering Layers

Now that we have two layers—one shape and one text layer—we can alter the hierarchy. Select the text layer and run the keyboard shortcut **cmd + option + ↓**. Our text layer has disappeared.

It's not hidden, but it *is* out of view, because we shifted it down one stage in the Layer List, and the rectangle layer now blocks its view. Press **cmd + option + ↑** to make it rise one level in the list. Now the layer appears as it did before.

1-9. Here, the text layer is hidden behind a rectangle layer because it appears lower in the list

Duplicating and Renaming Layers

Duplicating a layer can also be accomplished with the quick keyboard shortcut **cmd + D**—which makes much more sense than Photoshop's **cmd + J**.

Renaming layers is **cmd + R**.

Groups

We now know how to create, select, hide, reorder and duplicate layers, but what about entire components? In this context, a **component** is two or more layers that make up to something bigger. For example, a button background (rectangle shape layer) and button text (text layer) would make up a button component.

Layers can be combined into single components so that several related layers can be moved and aligned at once. These single components are called **groups**.

You can select multiple layers at once by holding **cmd** while clicking on their names in the Layer List (add **shift** into the mix if you're doing this from the canvas). Press **cmd + G** on the keyboard to combine those selected layers into a single group, which then adopts its own hierarchy as well as being *part* of another hierarchy.

A group can be selected and moved as if it were a single layer.

1-10. Our rectangle and text layers have been wrapped in a group, aptly named "Rectangle 1 + hello"

In the toolbar there's also a **Group** and **Ungroup** button.

Accessing Nested (Or "Child") Layers

Nested layers are layers that are wrapped inside a group. In order to select a layer inside a group, you first need to select the group and then double-click the layer inside it; otherwise you'll need to select it manually from the Layer List. Layers can be nested inside groups that are also nested inside other groups, which eventually makes layer selection quite tiresome.

We can bypass this need to double-click by selecting the group and checking the **Click-through when selecting** checkbox in the **Inspector**, which appears on the right-hand side of the UI.

You can accomplish the same thing by holding **cmd** while you click. It will allow you to directly click-through to the nested layer on a temporary basis—but due the simplicity of this feature, it's usually best to do it this way all the time.

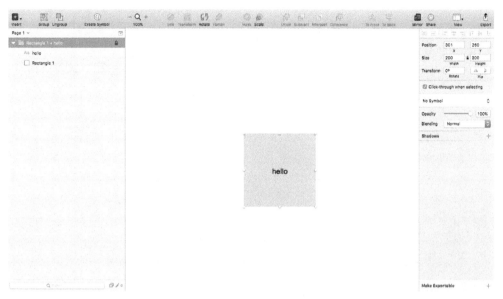

1-11. Directly click a nested layer by checking the "Click-through when selecting" box

Pages

Eventually, your canvas will start to build up, and you'll be responsible for many different layers and groups, as well as Artboards (which I'll talk about in the next chapter). As I mentioned earlier, there's no need to split a design into various files. In order to maintain cleanliness, we use Pages.

At the very top of the Layer List you'll notice that it says "Page 1". Press the icon (boxed-arrow) in the top right corner of the Layer List and then again to open a new "Page". If you wanted to separate your homepage from your about us section, for example, this would be an ideal way to do it. Keeping a neat .sketch file is a combined effort between groups, Artboards and Pages.

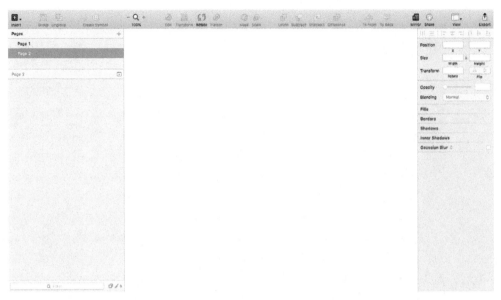

1-12. Sketch's "Pages" management tab

Renaming Pages

When focused on a layer or group in the Layer List, **cmd + R** lets you rename it easily. However, this doesn't work within the Pages tab, so you'll have to double-click to rename those. In order to distinguish between a homepage (for instance) and an About Us section, we can rename "Page 1" and "Page 2" to "Homepage" and "About us" respectively.

If you're following along with the steps I've described so far, make sure to revert back to "Homepage" before we move on, as that's what I'll focus on for the time being.

The Inspector

I mentioned above something called the **Inspector**, which appears on the right-hand side of the Sketch window. No, it's not an awesome comic book superhero; it's where we style our layers and declare optional settings for our Artboards and groups. If you're familiar with building websites in "Design view", you'll find this is exactly the same, only without the generated code.

Different types of layers have different options available to them. Groups and Artboards don't have any style options at all, but they do have *settings*. We'll explore this awesomely named Inspector in much more depth in Chapter 3. Don't disappear!

1-13. Sketch UI with the inspector visible

The Toolbar

In the **toolbar** (up top) you'll see a row of … well … tools. Each of these fulfills a specific action—most of which we'll discuss throughout the various chapters in this book, and some of which we've already discussed (such as Group, Ungroup, Forward and Backward). You may have noticed **Insert** too, which is an alternative way of inserting shapes, vectors and bitmaps.

In short, the toolbar offers quick access to some of the most-used tools in Sketch. We won't be able to cover every aspect of Sketch in this book (like vectoring, which is quite complex), but we will cover the vital tools that appear in this toolbar.

1-14. Sketch UI with the toolbar visible

Hiding the UI

Sometimes, especially if you're working on a tiny 11-inch MacBook Air like me, you'll want to take an objective look at your work without the user interface being in the way. You can toggle literally every aspect of the UI on and off with a shortcut:

- Layer List: **cmd + option + 1**
- Inspector: **cmd + option + 2**
- Toolbar: **cmd + option + T**

As you may have noticed, I've been doing this in some of the screenshots so they're cleaner and easier to understand.

Context Menu

Also known as the "right-click menu", the **context menu** changes its options depending on where you click. It's like an ever-changing tool menu that offers you tools relevant to the object in focus.

For instance, if you right-click on a layer, you'll be able to extract its style markup as CSS by clicking the **Copy CSS Attributes** option in the context menu. Many of the actions available in the context menu can also be accessed from the toolbar, or more often than not, a handy keyboard shortcut.

In rarer cases, you might have to dig through the app's native menu to access **File**, **Edit**, **Layer**, **Type**, **Arrange**, **Plugins** or **View**. However, the options and tools listed here aren't commonly used by most designers. Sketch's context menu aims to make some of those "hidden" tools more accessible.

Whether you choose to use the context menu or the menu bar is up to you. It mostly depends on how complex your needs are.

1-15. Sketch's context menu when hovered over a layer; some options are unique to layers

1-16. Different options are available if you right-click elsewhere—for example, the toolbar

Summary

What makes Sketch so wonderfully versatile is that many of the features can be found in the context menu, the toolbar *and* the menu bar, not to mention the fact that they're accessible via a keyboard shortcut too. You can use Sketch in a way that suits *you*. Let's sum up the core aspects of Sketch's user interface:

- Page: a fresh, blank canvas inside a *document*
- Canvas: a blank, unlimited workspace inside a *Page*
- Artboard: an optional template inserted into the *canvas*
- Layers: the shapes, text and bitmap images inside an *Artboard*
- Layer List: a list of groups and layers ordered by hierarchy
- Inspector: an interface for specifying styles and settings
- Toolbar: a row of mouse-operated design tools
- Menu bar: the native app menu for less common tools.

Chapter

2

Artboards, Layers, and Styling

In comparison to Adobe Photoshop, layers in Sketch tend to feel quite tangible—as if you could effortlessly mold them into shape with your fingers. Point-and-click actions are very smooth, even though keyboard shortcuts make up most of the interactions, and styling layers is a total breeze from start to finish.

In this chapter, we're going to discuss the magic of Artboards, as well as take a deeper look into the different types of layers and how we style them using the Inspector.

Artboards

If you've been using Photoshop almost exclusively up until now, you might not be too familiar with Artboards. Illustrator has used Artboards for years, but

Photoshop only added the functionality in 2015 in an effort to compete with Sketch.

Artboards are basically constraints, like a sized canvas within an unlimited canvas. Almost any design tool will allow you to create Artboards of a custom size, but it's more common to select a *predefined* size. For example, if you're designing an app for the iPhone 6 Plus, you would be able to create an Artboard of that size without having to know the correct dimensions. Sketch lets you do exactly this, with minimal effort.

But why are Artboards so important? Well, because Artboards set their own coordinate system origins, meaning **zero** on the X and Y axis originates from the top-left corner of each Artboard—which makes the task of aligning and sizing layers much easier if your unlimited canvas has more than the one Artboard. Having several Artboards on the canvas all at once means that we can keep an entire website design contained in a single .sketch file.

Artboards always display their name (in the canvas) above the top-left corner of the Artboard. Predefined Artboards will use the name of the device—for example, "Apple Watch 42mm". Just like with layers, **cmd + R** will let you rename Artboards.

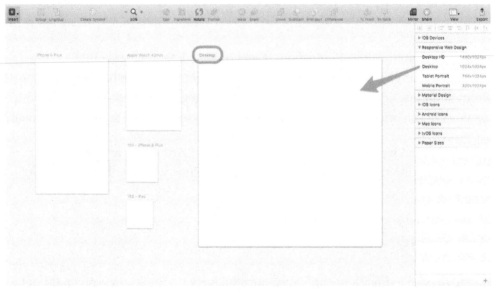

2-1. Artboards in action

Creating Artboards

Press **A** ("A" for Artboard) to make the Artboard tab appear in the Inspector. You'll see a list of devices here, and those devices indicate exactly what Sketch is meant for. When designing something that's not meant to be in a device frame, you can simply drag-create an Artboard as if it were an ordinary shape, effectively defining your own custom boundaries for the design.

 Making an Artboard Around a Layer

If you select a layer and *then* try to insert an Artboard, you'll have the option to create an Artboard "Around Selection".

Artboards are split into the following categories:

- iOS Devices
- Responsive Web Design
- Material Design
- iOS Icons
- Android Icons
- Mac Icons
- tvOS Icons
- Paper Sizes

Moving and Resizing Artboards

Like any other type of object in the canvas, Artboards can be selected, moved, resized, renamed and duplicated. However, moving and resizing can also be done from the Inspector, which is represented by a series of input fields. For Artboards, this is:

- Position: X
- Position: Y
- Size: Width
- Size: Height

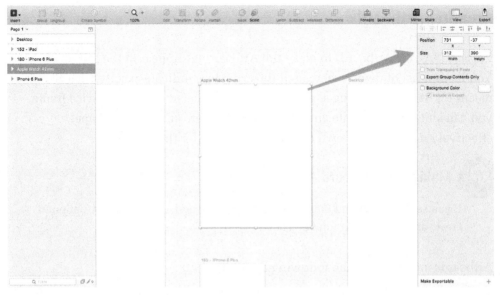

2-2. Repositioning and resizing Artboards using the Inspector

Resizing Artboards via Keyboard

You can resize Artboards (and layers as well) without the Inspector, by combining the keyboard arrow buttons with **cmd**.

Resizing Artboards to Fit the Content

You can hit the **Resize to Fit** button to trim the Artboard's whitespace.

Layers

So far, we've learned that the Inspector lets us … well … *inspect* objects in the canvas and make changes to them. Artboards don't have many editable options; they're simply the space we'll build our designs on. Layers are the building blocks of our design, and that's where styling becomes more exciting.

Before we learn more about styling layers, let's first create a shape layer inside an Artboard. Choose an "Apple Watch 38mm" Artboard and then select **R** for *Rectangle* on the keyboard.

Draw it out on the canvas.

2-3. A custom-sized, drawn-out rectangle ("Rectangle 1") in an Apple Watch 38mm Artboard

At this stage, we're not going to design anything useful, but instead explore the different styles and options available to each type of layer. In the following chapters, when we're more familiar with what Sketch can accomplish, we'll try our hand at designing something awesome, such as a complete web component.

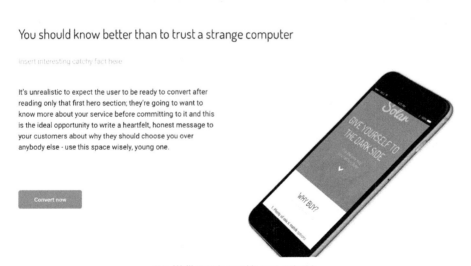

2-4. We'll start by working towards this

Maintaining Layer Aspect Ratio

Assuming you're still focused on the rectangle, tap **delete** on the keyboard to erase the layer from existence (not forever, of course). Let's try to create a *perfect* rectangle this time.

Hold **shift** while you drag-draw the rectangle to ensure a 1:1 ratio (i.e. a square). You'll know when "aspect ratio" is in effect because a closed lock will appear in between the *Width* and *Height* options in the Inspector. Drag-drawing shapes without **shift** means that no aspect ratio is maintained, but you can click the lock icon to toggle this on and off anyway.

Let's aim for 200x200px. If you couldn't achieve the accuracy required during the drag (sometimes zooming in helps), you can change the width and height settings in the Inspector.

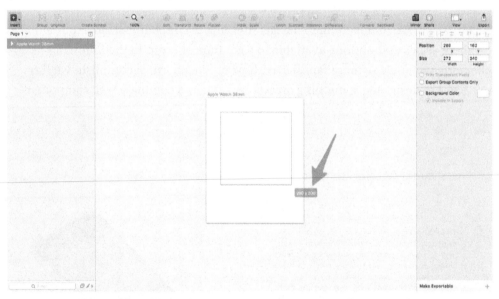

2-5. Holding **shift** mid-draw will ensure that the width and height of the shape are the same

Aligning and Snapping Layers

Drag the square into the center of the Artboard until the red Smart Guides appear, indicating that the square has "snapped" to the direct center. Smart Guides appear whenever a layer is in transit. We'll talk more about Smart Guides in Chapter 4.

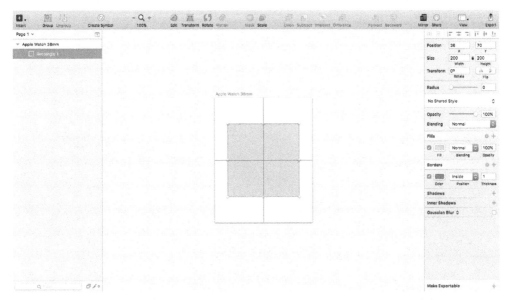

2-6. Rectangle 1 has been "snapped"

Can we align layers with the Inspector? Yes.

At the top of the Inspector there are eight icons that indicate a different type of alignment. You can use these buttons to align layers as well, but you'll find snapping easier most of the time.

2-7. Align objects with the Inspector

Styling Shape Layers

By default, fresh-on-the-canvas shape layers (like our rectangle) will be gray, and with a border. Let's walk through each styling option one by one, from top to bottom in the Inspector, excluding the styles we've already discussed (X, Y, Width and Height).

Jump Start Sketch doesn't assume you have any coding knowledge, since it's not a requirement for using Sketch. However, web developers will be happy to know that each style in the Inspector does have a CSS-equivalent attribute. For example, **Radius** in Sketch is represented as border-radius in CSS. Later in the chapter, we'll discuss how Sketch styles can be converted to CSS code.

The following styles available to shape layers:

- Rotate: specifies the angle of rotation from 0–360 degrees
- Flip: two buttons that mirror the layer horizontally/vertically
- Radius: creates rounded corners on rectangle shapes only
- Opacity: alters the transparency of the entire layer
- Blending: specifies the blending mode of the entire layer
- Fill: declares the background of the layer

- Borders: alters the color, box sizing and thickness of borders
- Shadows: creates a shadow around the layer
- Inner Shadows: creates a shadow *inside* the layer
- Blurs: four styles of blur for rare, special use cases

As a quick design exercise, let's convert our basic rectangle shape to a text-less button. Remember to turn off aspect ratio by clicking the lock icon and snap-align the layer into the dead center afterwards. You can use the following values/styles:

- Width: 180
- Height: 50
- Radius: 5

2-8. Our first styled layer

Styling Text Layers

Many of the styles that apply to shape layers also apply to text layers as well, but there's a few styles that are specific to text layers. Let's take a brief look at those, after first creating a text layer. Press **T**, click on the canvas, and type "button".

Now let's observe the Inspector once again:

- Typeface: specifies the font family of the text layer

- Weight: specifies the font weight
- Options: adds extra font styling such as bullets and underlines
- Color: changes the color of the text layer or *selected* text
- Alignment: four buttons that alter the text direction
- Width (Auto): makes the text layer fluid in width
- Width (Fixed): specifies a fixed width (for word wrapping)
- Spacing (Character): amount of space between letters
- Spacing (Line): adjusts the line height of the text
- Spacing (Paragraph): amount of space between new lines

In this case, use the following values/styles:

- Typeface: Helvetica
- Weight: Bold
- Color: White
- Size: 16
- Width: Auto

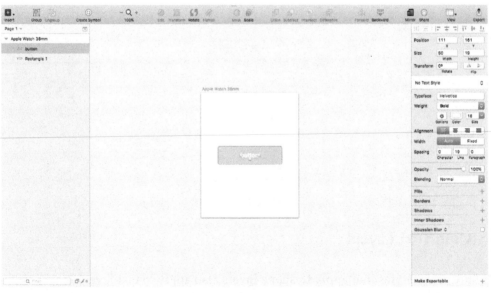

2-9. We almost have a button

Adding and Removing Styles from Layers

Color-based styles can be unchecked in the Inspector—either to compare a layer with or without the style, or to remove it indefinitely. If you no longer want the style at all, the mechanical cog icon that opens up the super-advanced options turns into a trash icon and we can then remove the style forever.

Since we don't want or need the default gray border of our rectangle shape, uncheck the checkbox that appears under **Borders**, and then click the trash icon to remove it completely.

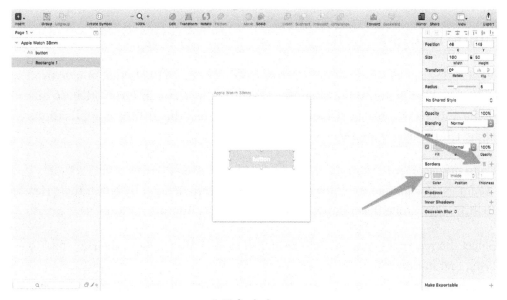

2-10. Border begone

 Adding Extra Layers

In the same way that layers can be removed, the + icon can do the exact opposite. Sometimes a single shadow isn't enough, for example, so you can use a combination of shadows to achieve the desired effect.

Incrementing Numerical Values with Shift-hold

For the styles that are defined by numerical values (such as Width) there's a speed hack called **shift-hold. Shift-hold** increments values in many ways across Sketch, and we'll talk about those instances as we approach them, but in this case holding **shift** while using the up and down arrows will make the values increment by 10 instead of 1—saving lots of time.

Mathematical Operations

Numerical input fields can also accept mathematical operations, so you don't have to know the desired width of a layer to be able to define it. Percentages are also welcomed—for example, "90%" will return 900px if the *parent* Artboard/group is 1000px.

Color Management

Most styles can be summed up in a few words. It's quite likely that you've used a design tool before (even if it wasn't Photoshop, Illustrator or Fireworks), so many of the options will feel very familiar, despite the fact that different applications approach the user experience in different ways.

Color management is simply a delight for Sketch users. We use the "Fill" or "Color" styles to manage color in Sketch. Colors are defined by either their **Hex** or **RGBA** value, since that's how devices and screens interpret colors.

Select the rectangle layer and click the **Fill** style. Put FF3654 in the **Hex** field to bring that button to life.

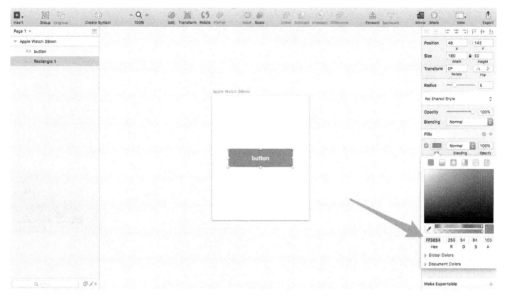

2-11. Our button has been "filled"

Extracting Color Values with the Eyedropper Tool

Eyedropper functions are used in all kinds of design tools to extract a specific color from the screen and use it elsewhere. They're quite straightforward but incredibly useful. Press the eyedropper icon in the color modal (above the Hex field) and hover the screen (yep, this works outside of the Sketch window too!) to bring out the magnifier, which can then be used to zoom in and extract color values from anywhere on the screen.

The keyboard shortcut for initiating the eyedropper tool is **control + C**.

2-12. Searching for a specific color

Press **esc** on the keyboard to exit the eyedropper tool, since we've already defined a stunning color for our button!

Frequent, Global and Document Colors

On the opposite side of the color modal, there's a box that initiates a drop-down when clicked. It's basically a list of colors that appear frequently throughout the document, saving you the time and effort of having to remember hex values.

So far we've only used two different colors, one for the button background (hex `ff3654`, or "radical") and another for the button text (white).

2-13. Our frequently used colors

At the bottom of the modal, there's a range of random colors under the **Global Colors** tab. These appear in every Sketch document, and they're all yours for the taking. **Document Colors**, on the other hand, will be empty, but there is a + sign that lets you add the currently selected color to this roster.

Do this with the radical color.

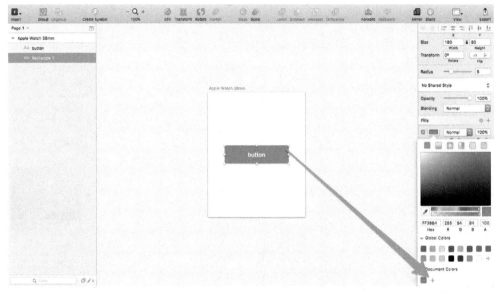

2-14. Saving our radical color for later

If you open a new Sketch document, this roster will be reset, because document colors are colors chosen *by you* for quick use in the *current* document only. Generally, it's a time-saving technique to save all of your branding and user interface colors in this roster so they can be accessed with ease later on.

 Tidying Up the UI

> If you don't use this function often, you can collapse the two tabs, since it makes the user interface look a little cleaner.

Linear Gradients

At the very top of the modal there are several rounded-corner icons that depict different types of fill. Adjacent to **Flat Colors** (the exact name of the fill is revealed if you hover the icon) is **Linear Gradient**, which is represented on the canvas by two selectable color stops. Each stop *is* a color, and the transitional fade occurs between those stops, where more stops can be added by clicking on the connecting line between them.

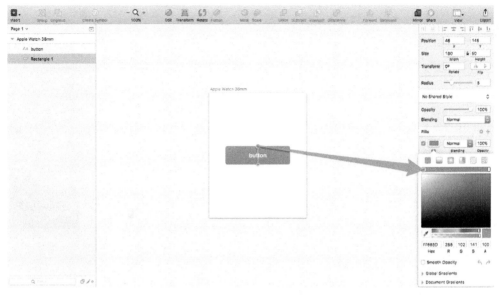

2-15. Fading occurs between the two stops

Sketch users mostly create and move the color stops with the mouse, but there's also a slider that mimics some of the capabilities of the canvas way of doing things. A huge benefit to directly interacting with the color stops on the canvas is that we have access to keyboard shortcuts that make things easier:

- **=**: new stop will center between the two adjacent stops
- **1–9**: new stop will reposition at exactly 10–90%
- **tab**: quickly toggles between color stops

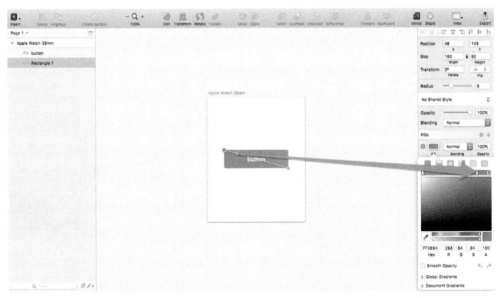

2-16. Here, the color transition occurs diagonally, with an extra stop specifically inserted at 20%

 Tweaking the Transitions

If the colors are transitioning in the wrong direction, there are two arrows in the color management modal that can invert them, and the **Smooth Opacity** checkbox offers smoother transitioning between multiple color stops. (If you haven't added any extra stops, this has no effect whatsoever.)

Radial Gradients and **Angular Gradients** work almost the same way. In the case of our button, though, I think we'll leave it flat (because we're oh-so-trendy). Flick back to the flat color version, which Sketch has thoughtfully remembered for us.

Context Menu

We spoke about the context menu in Chapter 1. It's a very convenient way of accessing hidden gem features (that are otherwise buried deep in the app's menu) with a simple right-click—and there are two excellent ones that apply to layers.

Sketch to CSS

As I've mentioned in this chapter already, styling layers in Sketch is very CSS-centric, so it's not surprising that you can extract CSS styles. All you need to do is right-click, select **Copy CSS Attributes**, and the styles will be copied to the clipboard, ready for you to use in your coded website designs.

Here's what was extracted from "Rectangle 1".

```
/* Rectangle 1: */
  background: #FF3654;
  border-radius: 5px;
```

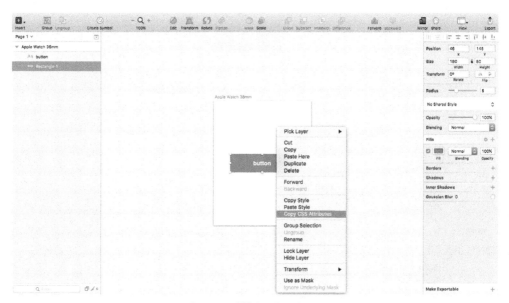

2-17. Extracting CSS data from Rectangle 1

Copying and Pasting Layers

Paste has always been a universal feature. We use it for a variety of media and in a variety of applications. In design tools, however, we'd like to be a lot more specific in regards to how we copy layers, and that's where the context menu comes in:

- Copy: **cmd + C**
- Paste: **cmd + P**

Paste Here becomes available when you open the context menu from the canvas, where the object is inserted directly underneath the mouse cursor. **Paste Over**, on the other hand, can be accessed when opening the context menu from the Layer List, and the object is inserted from the top-left corner of the selected layer.

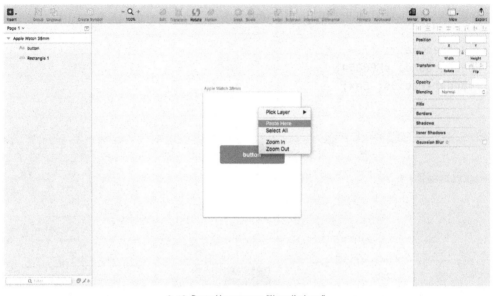

2-18. Paste Here means "literally here"

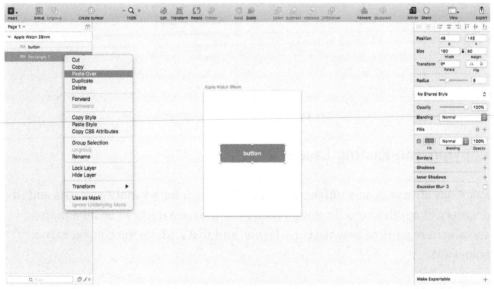

2-19. Paste Over means "on top of this layer"

Versioning

Sketch has autosave functionality that saves your work at regular intervals. When it's switched on (the default setting), you can use **File → Revert To → Browse All Versions...** to visualize your `.sketch` file through time. For minor mistakes, the regular **Undo** and **Redo** shortcuts work reliably enough:

- Undo: **cmd + Z**
- Redo: **cmd + shift + Z**

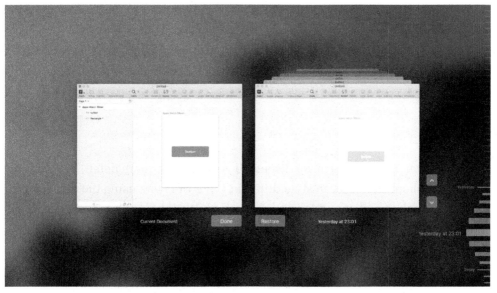

2-20. Previous and current versions of our button component design displayed side by side

By using the mouse wheel or the up/down buttons, you can select an earlier version of the document and revert back to it.

You can also switch off autosave by navigating to **Sketch → Preferences** in the menu bar, or by using the keyboard shortcut **cmd + ,**. (Before autosave became optional, many designers requested the option to turn it off, because they were sometimes making experimental changes and forgetting that autosave was saving those changes.) Personally, I think it's dangerous to turn autosave off, because you never know when an application might crash. I wouldn't recommend switching it off, ever.

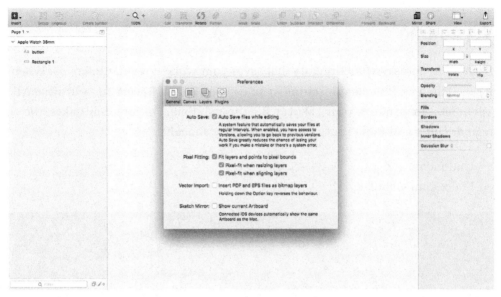

2-21. Autosave can be turned off

Summary

In this chapter, not only have we discussed Artboards in more detail, but we've also talked about how we can style different types of layers using the Inspector, and revert back to earlier versions when needed. We'll be using our button design in the next chapter, so make sure you don't throw it away.

Chapter 3 will be a whole other story. We'll learn how to use Shared Styles and symbols to our advantage, saving us bundles of time by reusing common elements over and over again.

Chapter **3**

Shared Styles and Symbols

You might be familiar with Cascading Style Sheets (CSS), the coding language that developers use to style websites. Sketch's own styling deeply resembles CSS, and as we saw in Chapter 2, Sketch can even convert its own styling into CSS for us.

However, Sketch's beautiful friendship with web design doesn't end there. This chapter will explore the ways in which we can keep multiple layers (or blocks of layers) consistent by making the styles reusable, so that when you want to change the look of recurring elements—such as buttons—you only need to do it once.

It works like this for individual layers:

1. you create a layer and style it
2. you make it reusable (it's now called a **Shared Style**)

3. you duplicate it however many times
4. you restyle one of the layers
5. but the changes are applied to all layers

And like this for blocks (of layers):

1. you create multiple layers and style them
2. you select all of the layers at once
3. you make the layers reusable (they're now called a **symbol**)
4. you duplicate the symbol however many times
5. you restyle a single instance of the symbol
6. but the changes are applied to all instances of the symbols

Why Shared Styles and Group Symbols Exist

Shared Styles and symbols allow you to reuse styles (or entire components) over and over again. Since visual interfaces rely on consistency and familiarity to offer an optimal user experience, learning how to reuse common design components and shave valuable seconds off your workflow should become second nature to you when designing with Sketch. Let's take a look at some examples:

- **Shared Styles** can be used to keep all headings in a design looking consistent with the same font family, size and color.

- **Symbols** can be used to keep a block of layers (such as a button background and its companion text) consistent, should your website have multiple instances of that button design.

In this chapter, we'll dig even deeper and begin exploring these Shared Styles and symbols, and the many ways that they can save huge amounts of time. What we have here are two wonderfully complementary features that illustrate exactly why Sketch is the ultimate tool for user interface design. And just as the Sketch styles are so elegantly attuned with CSS styles, Shared Styles and symbols behave in a very CSS-like manner as well.

How Shared Styles and Symbols Relate to CSS

I won't delve too far into CSS, since that's not really what *Jump Start Sketch* is about, but those that do code may find the comparisons interesting. CSS has something called "classes".

Classes are a way of defining many styles under a single name. For example, a button with a blue background, rounded corners, a subtle box shadow and a width of 180px may be used several times throughout a website (for consistency), and so we can create a class aptly named "button" and reuse this button multiple times, as opposed to rewriting the actual styles over and over again.

Shared Styles and symbols follow a similar concept. If you still have our button component from Chapter 2, hold **cmd** while you click the layers in the Layer List (to select them both simultaneously) and copy them (**cmd + C**) to the clipboard.

Setting Up a New Document and Artboard

Now open a new Sketch document (**cmd + N**) and create a new Artboard (**A**). Select the "Desktop HD" Artboard under **Responsive Web Design** and then use **Paste Here** from the context menu. Paste it near the bottom-left of the Artboard.

3-1. Our new "Desktop HD" Artboard

Creating Reusable Elements

Since we already have a button design, we'll start with symbols.

Creating Symbols

Select both layers again and choose **Create Symbol** from the toolbar. A dialog will appear asking you to name this symbol: call it "Red Button". You should also make sure that the **Send Symbols to Symbols Page** option is checked. When the .sketch document acquires its first symbol (and this option is checked), a new page called "Symbols" will be automatically created.

3-2. Creating a symbol

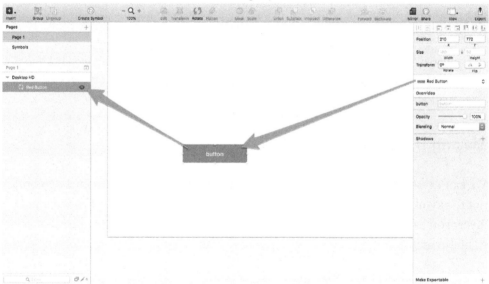

3-3. Symbol created

 ## Maintainability

If you choose not to send symbols to the symbols page, they will appear in the current page alongside your actual designs, which is fine, but having all of your symbols in a dedicated canvas will certainly make your document easier to maintain.

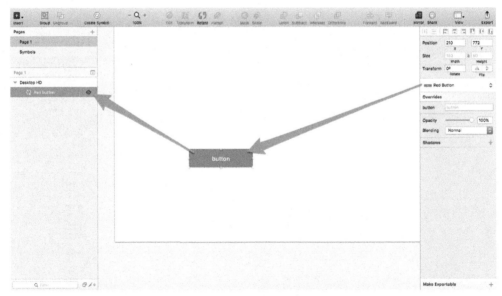

3-4. "Red Button", our first symbol

Shared Styles and Symbols Are Color-Coded

Shared Styles and symbols have *purple* icons in the Layer List. If an icon is blue, then it's a regular layer with no symbol assigned to it, or a regular layer that isn't sharing any styles

Making Document-wide Changes

We can't restyle this button here. What we have here is an *instance* of a symbol, not the symbol itself. Instances are versions of the symbol flattened into a single layer; you can move the instance around, duplicate it, or create more instances of it, but to edit it you'll have to switch to the symbols page.

Duplicate (**cmd + D**) this instance of the symbol.

3-5. One symbol, two instances

Now switch to the symbols page. You'll notice that our red button exists here, unflattened, and with all of its original layers intact. *This* is the symbol. We can edit this symbol and the changes will automatically synchronize with every other instance in the document. Change the **Fill** color to something else.

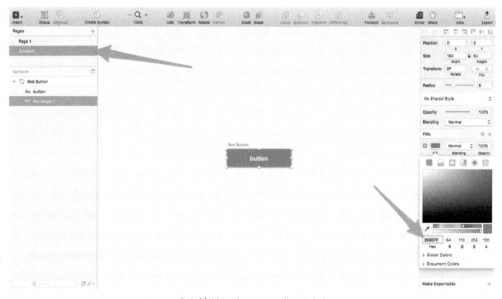

3-6. Making changes to the symbol

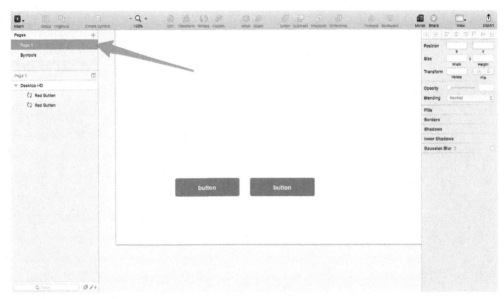

3-7. Instances are immediately updated

 ## Symbols Are Always Identical

Symbols in Sketch are *always* identical—no exceptions. If you have a collection of "symboled" components and one of them suddenly needs to look even a *little* different, then it needs to be either a *new* symbol or not a symbol at all.

Symbol Overrides

Like I said, there sadly isn't an "always keep these buttons consistent except for the background" option. If you need a secondary button (for less important calls to action, maybe) and it needs to be a different color, then you must create a new symbol for it. But that being said, you *can* override text (and even images) so that each instance can have unique content.

So undo (**cmd + Z**) the changes until both buttons are red again and select one of the instances. Observe the "Overrides" tab in the Inspector: you'll see that the text value has an input field next to it. You can replace the text value in this instance by typing something else into this field. If you have an image inside a symbol, you can accomplish the same thing, essentially offering unique content to each instance of the reusable symbol.

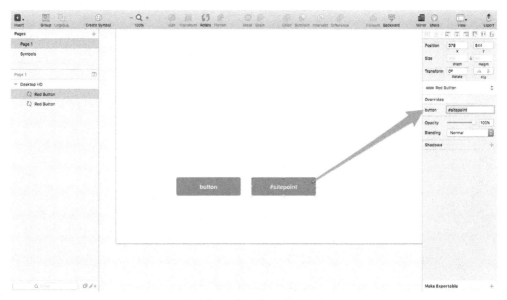

3-8. Overwriting the default text

I can't think of anything worse than finishing what I consider to be a splendid web design, only to have the client request changes that will take forever to fix. Well, with Sketch, we can not only make super-fast changes to multiple identical elements at once, but there's also a degree of flexibility in the actual *content*.

Detaching from a Symbol

If you need to detach an instance from a symbol, maybe because you need to make visual changes, select **Detach from Symbol** in the Inspector. You can also do this from the context menu. After that, you can create and attach a new symbol to it.

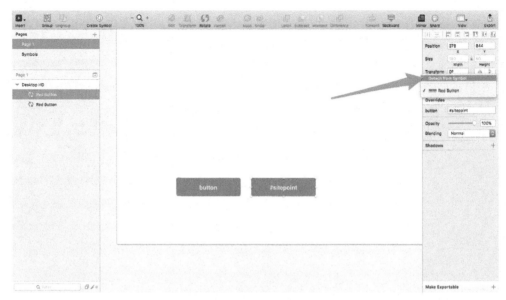

3-9. Detaching an instance from a symbol

Inserting a New Instance Into the Canvas

When you start to accumulate the majority share of your symbols, designing with Sketch turns into *building* with Sketch. Select **Insert → Symbol** to populate the canvas with your symbols.

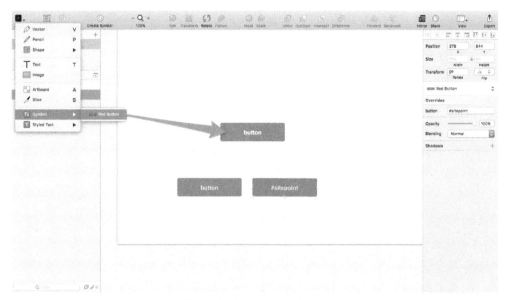

3-10. Inserting instances into the canvas

Shared Styles and Text Styles

Sketch has something called **Shared Styles** and **Text Styles** as well, and these apply to individual shape layers and text layers respectively. Shared Styles don't differ from Text Styles at all really; we only call them Text Styles for clarity.

What sets Shared Styles and Text Styles apart from group symbols is the level of stretchability—meaning they can have completely unique dimensions but otherwise be identical. For this reason, when you extract styles from a layer as CSS code, you'll notice that the width and height attributes are always omitted from the output.

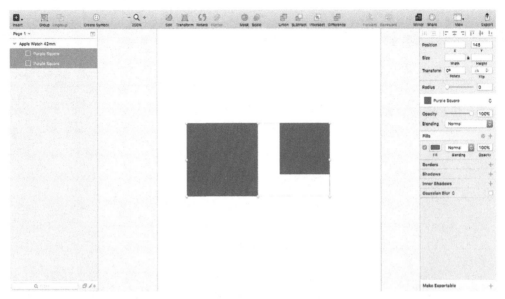

3-11. Both of these layers are attached to the same Shared Style, but have unique dimensions

Before we advance with our design, it's important to understand when Shared/ Text Styles should be chosen over symbols, and how to organize them as our .sketch file becomes more elaborate.

Knowing When to Create Symbols

It's quite easy to assume that whenever you have a component that appears in the document more than once, it should be a symbol, but that isn't true (especially with smaller components).

Due to their lack of suppleness, you could end up with way too many symbols to look after, and in this case it may be more beneficial to mix and match Shared Styles instead—which will require less maintenance and more offer options. For the record, you absolutely can have Shared/Text Styles *inside* symbols. (You can even have nested symbols—that is, symbols inside symbols.)

Consider a website design with many different button styles. Ghost buttons, filled buttons, with shadow, without shadow, rounded corners, sharp corners, small, medium, large; a button might be any combination of these, and a collection of reusable elements (consisting of both Shared Styles and Text Styles) lets us create any combination of button background and text.

You may even decide that fixed-width buttons are not right for your design, and so the use of symbols would not be useful here. It all comes down to one simple question: "If I needed to reuse this section later, what might I want to change?"

Forward-thinking Style Guides with Sketch

Early on in the design, there are a lot of firsts: first icon, first heading, first caption and so on. These are the sort of design elements that we may wish to keep consistent throughout our design. Each "first" is a forward-thinking opportunity to assign a Shared/Text Style to those elements at an early stage.

It's sort of like defining a small *style guide* to stick to throughout the course of our design, especially since font styles and families tend to be rather consistent in interface design.

Let's continue designing our desktop component. In this quick exercise, we'll iterate over reusable elements and also build up our Artboard so that we have more layers to work with in the next chapter. For the time being, we'll focus on Text Styles.

Press **T** to create a text layer and use the following options:

- Value: "You should know better than to trust a strange computer"
- Typeface: I downloaded and used "Dosis"
- Weight: Regular
- Color: 333
- Size: 36
- Width: Auto

Now select **No Text Style → Create New Text Style** from the Inspector and call it "Heading Default 3". On darker backgrounds, you'd want to invert the color to white, which is why the Text Style is referred to as "Heading Default 3" and not "Heading 3" (always think ahead when coming up with a naming convention).

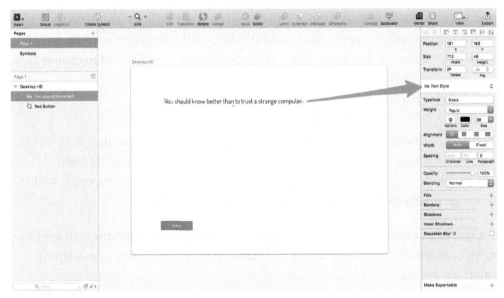

3-12. Our first reusable style

Repeat these steps with a Text Style called "Paragraph Faint":

- Value: "Insert interesting catchy fact here"
- Typeface: Helvetica
- Weight: Light
- Color: 999
- Size: 20
- Width: Auto

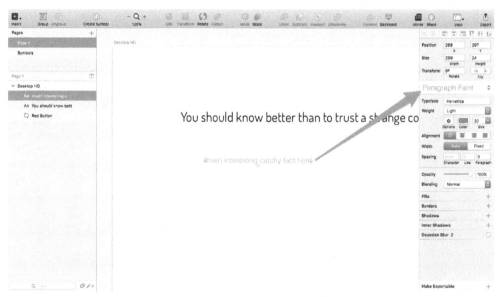

3-13. Our second reusable style

Finally, once more with "Paragraph Default":

- Value: any dummy text will do
- Width: 560
- Typeface: Helvetica
- Weight: Regular
- Color: 333
- Size: 20
- Width: Fixed

3-14. Our final reusable style

Removing Redundant Shared/Text Styles

You can select **Organise Text Styles** from that same dropdown menu in the Inspector, and then click the minus icon to remove a Text Style from the document; this works with Shared Styles too.

3-15. Removing unwanted reusable styles

How to Override Styles in Shared/Text Styles

Shared Styles and Text Styles don't have an override interface in the Inspector like symbols do, but there certainly is a huge deal of flexibility in their use. Symbols only allow you to override content. However instances of Shared Styles and Text Styles won't synchronise until you click the update icon in the Inspector, meaning you can have reusable styles with certain exceptions.

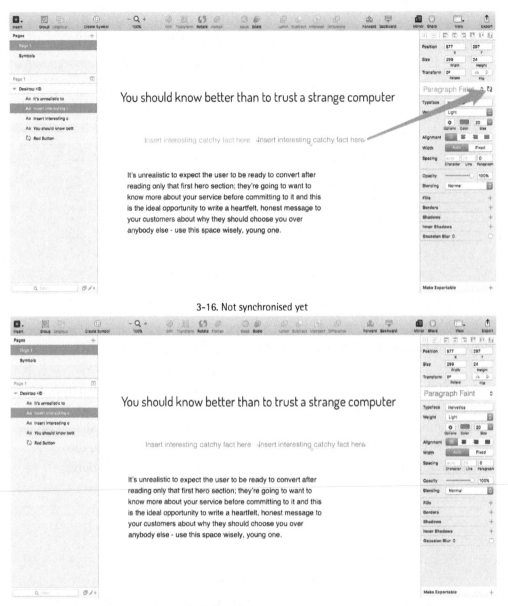

3-16. Not synchronised yet

3-17. Now they're synchronised

Summary

Shared Styles and symbols aid us in our effort to keep our designs uniform, so that we don't end up with too many styles and ultimately confuse our users when they view our interfaces. It's one of the many ways Sketch truly understands the needs of user interface designers.

In the next chapter, we'll explore another feature that has changed the way we design for screens—namely, Smart Guides.

Chapter

4

Smart Guides and Snapping

At the beginning of Chapter 1, I spoke briefly about invisible interfaces and how Smart Guides are an excellent example of that. Smart Guides inform the user of the distance between the current layer and another layer while moving it, or upon request by using a keyboard shortcut. With the exception of this keyboard shortcut (which is simply **option**), Smart Guides appear whenever Sketch thinks you need them—which is basically whenever a layer is in transit (i.e. dragging, moving or nudging).

Smart Guides appear when you:

- **drag** a layer with the mouse
- **move** a layer by 1px with the keyboard arrows (up, down, left or right)
- **nudge** a layer by 10px by combining **shift** with the keyboard arrows
- hold **option** and hover a different layer

What Do Smart Guides Look Like?

Smart Guides consist of solid, red lines.

Both layers being compared will have a red outline, and there will be another red line connecting the two layers. In the middle of this connecting line will be the numerical value indicating the space between the two layers. These red lines are the Smart Guides.

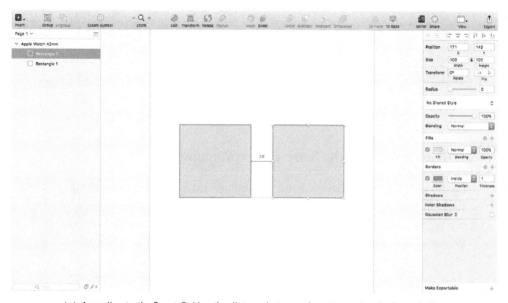

4-1. According to the Smart Guides, the distance between these two rectangle shapes is 30px

Sometimes (when comparing layers with Smart Guides using **option-hold**) a *dashed* line with no numerical equivalent will appear. Dashed lines simply clarify what layer you're comparing to, which is quite useful when your document contains many layers, and/or the two layers being compared are far apart.

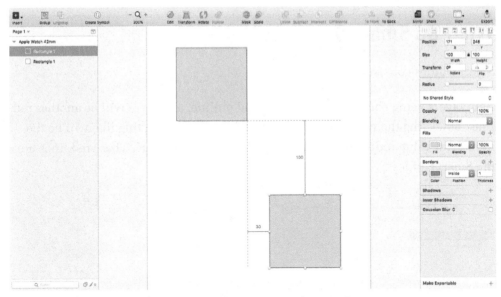

4-2. Dashed lines clarify which layer you're comparing to

Alignment is Not the Same as Text Alignment

By the way, alignment (meaning to "line up") in the context of Smart Guides shouldn't be confused with **text alignment**. In any chapter of this book, when we say "align", we're talking about how one layer measures up to another layer. Whenever we discuss the alignment/direction of text, I'll make it very clear.

Most of the time, you'll be aligning layers relative to other layers, but the existence of Artboards means that we can align layers relative to the Artboard edges as well. In more complex cases, you'll be able to specify Layout Settings and Grid Settings, and align layers in accordance to either one.

But we'll talk about that later. For now, open the artwork we created in Chapter 3 so that we can elaborate on it.

When Smart Guides Are Activated

Smart Guides are automatically activated when a layer is in transit—such as when you move, nudge, or drag a layer across the canvas. You can also force them to appear by holding **option**.

Let's take a look.

When Dragging

Layers will automatically snap to the edges of other layers and Artboards when you drag them, but that's not all. If the layer on the opposite side is (for example) 83px away, the layer in transit will snap to the middle layer at 83px as well. This is how Sketch's intuition helps you keep your spacing consistent.

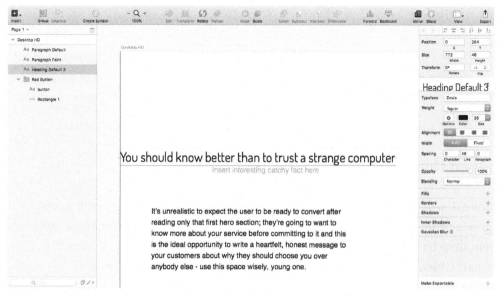

4-3. In this example, the layer in transit is snapping to both the Artboard edges and another layer

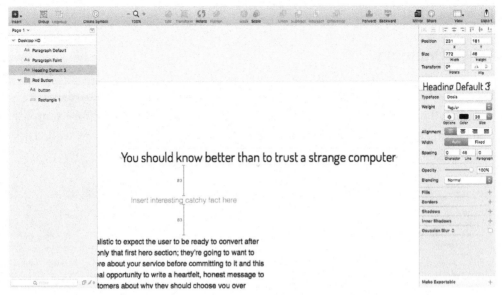

4-4. But here, however, Sketch is trying to keep the spacing between the two layers consistent

When Holding "Option"

Sometimes, you might want to obtain the "distance data" without ever actually moving a layer at all, and that's where **option-hold** comes in. Selecting a layer and then holding **option** while hovering over *another* layer will activate the Smart Guides, which then tells you how far apart those two layers are.

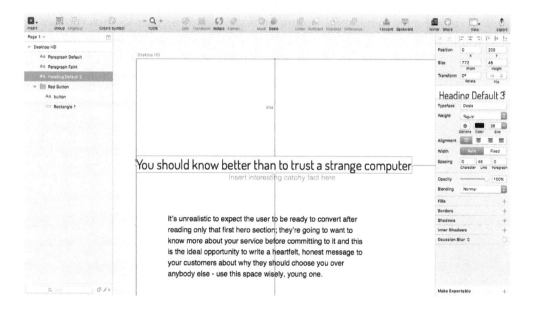

If you select more than one layer at once, Smart Guides will treat those layers like a group, and instead offer you the relative distance data of the total combined dimensions.

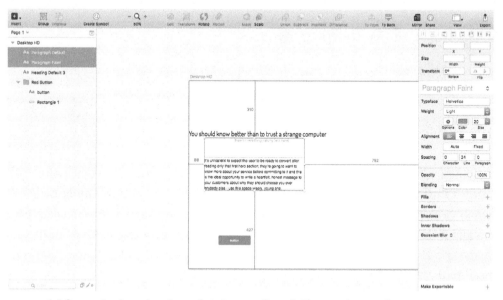

4-5. Because two layers have been selected at once, Smart Guides treat these two layers as a group

Do you remember what we learned about layer hierarchy back in Chapter 1? If you need to compare the distance between nested layers (that is, layers inside groups), you'll need to combine **option-hold** with **cmd** in order to click through the group. Otherwise, Smart Guides will offer you the distance between the entire group, rather than the layer *inside* the group.

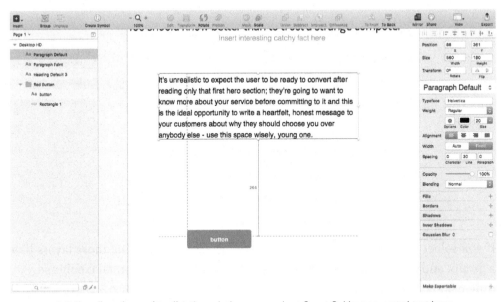

4-6. Here, I'm using **cmd** to click through the group and use Smart Guides on a nested text layer

 Non-intuitive Functionality

Holding **option** while dragging a layer actually duplicates the layer; it doesn't activate Smart Guides like you might think.

When Moving or Nudging

Moving isn't the same as dragging. **Moving** means you're using the keyboard arrows (instead of the mouse or Inspector) to reposition layers, and **nudging** is when you're incrementing the distance by 10 by holding **shift**. We used **shift** to increment values back in Chapter 2 when we discussed styling layers with the Inspector. Holding **shift** to increment values is a universal feature that can be used in a variety of ways.

But how does this relate to Smart Guides? Well, when you need to move layers by a larger amount, nudging makes this quicker, so it's common to combine **shift-**

hold with **option-hold** to increment by 10 and monitor the distance/movement simultaneously.

Let's try it out and begin aligning the layers in our `.sketch` document. Select the heading layer ("Heading Default 3"), hold **shift** and **option** together, and use the arrow buttons on the keyboard until the layer is **150px** from the top of the Artboard, and **135px** from the left side of the Artboard.

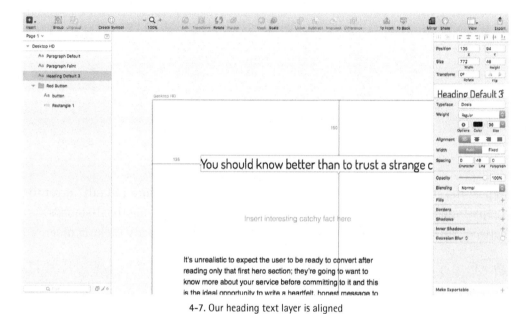

4-7. Our heading text layer is aligned

Do it again with the next text layer ("Paragraph Faint"). It also needs to be **135px** from the left side of the Artboard, but **30px** apart from "Heading Default 3". Since the layer will snap to the heading layer vertically, dragging will be the easiest way forward. You can use the directional buttons on the keyboard to fine-tune the offset if you're shaky with a mouse.

4-8. Snapping and aligning to nearby layers

Repeat the steps once more so that Sketch snaps the "Paragraph Default" layer to **135px** from the left side and **30px** from the above layer, keeping the distances between all layers wonderfully consistent. Our design is already looking nicer.

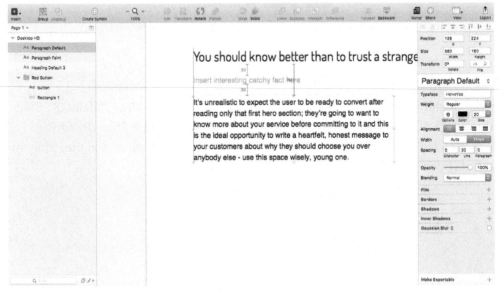

4-9. Snapping is intuitively consistent

Actually, we want to move "Paragraph Default" down another **20px**, but instead of using the directional arrows to move the layer down 1px at a time, hold **shift** to move it down by 10px at a time; this is how we use nudging to save a few seconds.

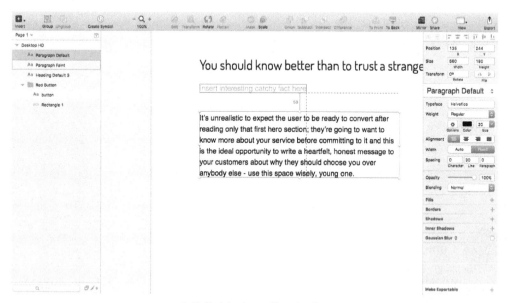

4-10. Nudging layers 10px at a time

As a final exercise, drag the button (yep, the entire group) until it snap-aligns with the other layers on the left side, and also so that it appears **100px** below"Paragraph Default".

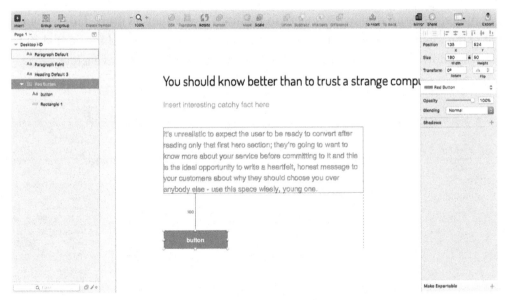

4-11. Fully-aligned at last!

Combining Keyboard Shortcuts and Features

By holding **option**, **shift** and **cmd** you can activate Smart Guides, move the layer by 10px at a time *and* click through to a nested layer all at once. Sketch is marvelous at keeping keyboard shortcuts simple so that you can combine several useful features together to create a highly energetic workflow.

Summary

It may seem as if this chapter has been the easiest, and you might be right, but it's also been the most eye-opening—at least it was for me when I first learned about Smart Guides.

Sketch's features are so simple, it makes you wonder why no other design tool has tried these types of features in such a way until now. Photoshop began introducing Smart Guides in its CC 2014 update, and that update also included a number of other features inspired by Sketch. Before this, Smart Guides existed only in our minds, where we had to count the number of "moves" mentally, rather than visually. Sketch made them a reality.

In the next chapter, we'll learn two things—how to work with bitmap images, and how to bend vector shapes to our will to create new shapes. Manipulating vectors isn't such a big deal in web design, since the web consists mostly of rectangles and sometimes circles. Shape manipulation mainly refers to icon design.

During the chapter, we'll wrap up the component that we've designed, and then start a new one in the same document.

Chapter 5

Vector and Bitmap Editing Tools

Layer manipulation falls into two categories: **vectors** and **bitmaps**. Vectors can be scaled to any size without losing quality, making it easy to export a design multiple times in different sizes—for example, when you need to support both Retina and non-Retina screens. The same, however, doesn't apply to bitmaps. You may be able to scale bitmaps *down* in size without losing too much quality, but you certainly won't be able to scale them up.

Sketch leans drastically towards being a vector app, which means that it only has a handful of bitmap tools. More often than not, you'll be importing *finished* bitmaps into the canvas, rather than using Sketch to create them—for example, when your website needs a detailed background or a device mockup.

Adobe Photoshop (or an alternative bitmap editing tool such as Affinity Photo) would be the ideal tool for creating and editing complex bitmap images. After that, we can import these bitmaps into our Sketch canvas to be used in our design mockups.

Editing vectors in Sketch is a lot easier. Most of the time, you'll be using vectors in the form of basic shapes, like we did when we created the rectangle base of our button. But when it comes to icon design or simple illustrations, rectangles and ovals won't cut it. You'll need to create *custom* shapes.

In this chapter, we'll discuss the features that let us use bitmap images in Sketch, as well as the tools that allow us to create vector shapes outside the boundaries of rectangles and ovals.

We'll continue from where we left off in the last chapter.

Resizing, Rotating and Scaling Layers

Let's start with something really simple—resizing and rotating layers. Rotation is defined by a measurement (degrees), so it's likely that you've already taken a quick look at rotating a layer from the Inspector. However, all bitmap and vector editing tools can be accessed from the toolbar, so **Rotate** appears there too.

Begin by creating a new rectangle (**Insert** → **Shape** → **Rectangle** or **R** on the keyboard) and moving it towards the empty area of the canvas. While the layer is still selected, observe the eight square handles that surround the edges of it. These square handles allow us to resize and rotate the layer without using the Inspector *or* the toolbar. Like I said back in the Chapter 2, layers in Sketch are quite tangible in comparison to Photoshop, in the sense that you can transform layers by grabbing and twisting them—as if you were using your hands.

5-1. Eight "pullable" handles

Resizing

You can make layers bigger or smaller by dragging the square handles outward or inward respectively. Which handle you select depends on which direction you want to resize in, unless you hold **option**, which forces the layer to resize from the center.

You can also hold **shift** to maintain the aspect ratio.

 Mouse Resizing

> Being able to do this manually (instead of using the Inspector) is useful for when you have only a mental idea of how large something should be. We call this method **mouse resize**.

In order to resize layers like the Inspector does (without actually using the Inspector), hold **cmd** while moving the directional arrows on the keyboard. This will save you from having to toggle through the input fields, although you'll still be able to notice the values changing in the Inspector. Layers will resize by 1px at a time, but you can hold **shift** to change the increment amount from 1px to 10px. When using this method, layers will scale from the left and bottom sides.

- Increase width: **cmd +** →
- Decrease width: **cmd +** ←
- Increase height: **cmd +** ↓
- Decrease height: **cmd +** ↑

Rotating

Rotate is another feature that can be accessed from the Inspector if you know the exact amount you'd like to rotate a layer by. If not, hold **cmd** and hover the handles to switch from **Resize** mode to **Rotate** mode. Simply drag the handles to rotate the layer (in a similar manner to resize).

Remember, you can still access **Rotate** (as well as many other tools) from the toolbar: you don't need to master keyboard shortcuts to master Sketch. Pick the method that suits you best.

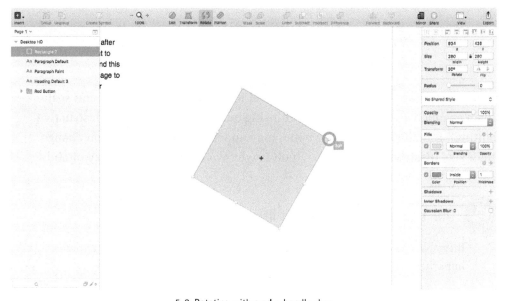

5-2. Rotating with **cmd** + handle-drag

Scaling

Scale can only be accessed from the toolbar, and it works a little bit differently from **Resize**. **Resize** changes the dimensions of a layer while keeping all of the other styles intact, but **Scale** also increases (or decreases) border and shadow widths relative to the level of scale. If a layer has a 1px border, for example, and you scale it up by 200%, the layer will be twice as large and the border will be 2px, like so:

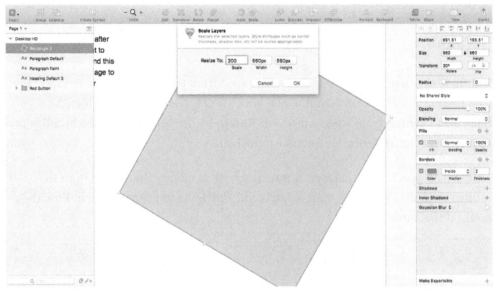

5-3. Scaling by 200%

Since vectors are formed by mathematical formulas, you can resize and scale them as much as you'd like without losing quality (known as **non-destructive** editing). Bitmaps, on the other hand, may appear distorted when you change their size (**destructive** editing), which is why we don't use them very often in Sketch.

Don't Try to Tweak Bitmaps after Importing Them

Bitmaps are very "final". It's better to not have to tweak them after copying or importing them into the document.

Transforming

In design, "transform" has a specific meaning, despite the term being quite vague in other contexts. When we say **transform**, we mean to skew or distort. When using **Transform** (which, again, appears in the toolbar), the handles will be circular, and the movement of those handles will be restricted, allowing you to remodel the shape only in a way that either skews or distorts it.

CSS Transforms are very similar to transforms in Sketch.

Skewing

Skewing allows you to transform a shape by slanting it at an angle. In order to skew a shape, you have to select **Transform** in the toolbar and then select one of the non-corner handles of the shape. In the example below, I've reverted the rotation back to the default and skewed the shape to the left.

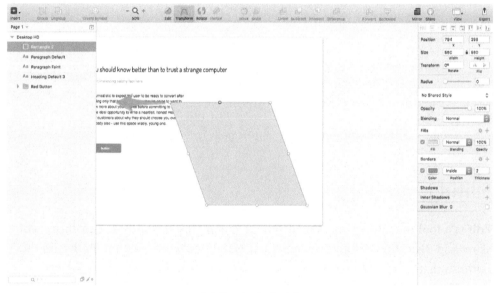

5-4. Skewing to the left

Distorting

Distorting can be accomplished by selecting one of the corner handles and prying it out of shape. By default, the reshaping occurs symmetrically, in an effort to conserve a degree of *perspective*—which results in a shape that might appear to be 3D, even if it isn't. However, by holding **cmd** while dragging a corner handle, we can distort the shape in a singular direction, as if to twist it rather than change its viewpoint.

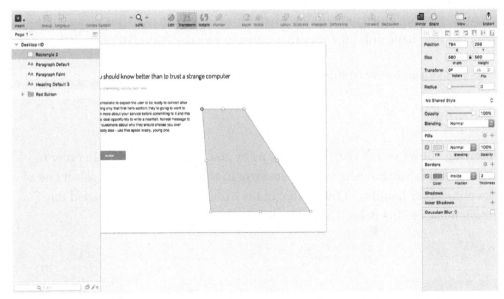

5-5. Perspective can be altered by distorting a shape with the Transform tool's corner handles

 Transforming and Rotating Bitmaps

Rotate and Transform work exactly the same way for bitmaps.

Editing

Edit is a tool that allows us to manipulate vectors (far beyond the capabilities of skew and distortion) by accessing the paths that make up a vector. **Paths** are the *outlines* that form a vector shape. Paths define the intervals of a vector—for example, when the line of a rectangle stops and does a right angle. We call that stop a **path point**, **anchor point**, or simply **point**.

A rectangle's path has four points, for example. If you delete a single point from a rectangle's path, it becomes a triangle. If you delete two points from a rectangle's path, you'll have a simple line. Paths are mathematically calculated, making them independent of resolution (and thus making them vectors).

Press **return** to activate **Edit** mode, or select it from the toolbar.

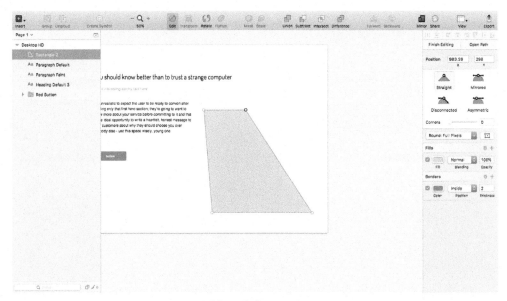

5-6. Edit mode for vector layers

Adding and Deleting Points

Straight away you should notice the four points of our rectangle shape at each corner of the path. You can select any one of these points and drag it around the canvas to transform the shape freely. You'll also notice a fresh interface in the Inspector—the basics of which we'll cover in this chapter.

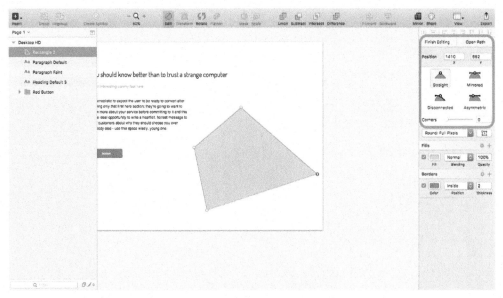

5-7. Dragging points freely

Hover along the line between any two points. It will appear navy blue, indicating that a new point can be added directly under your mouse cursor. Press **delete** to remove the point.

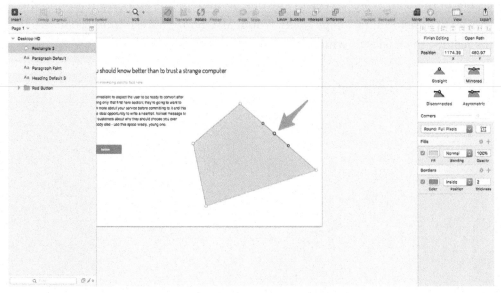

5-8. Adding a new point

Bézier Curves

Bézier curves sound fancy—because they are!—but I'll skip the technical definition[1] to make it less confusing. In short, **bézier curves** are *curved lines*. If you want curved lines instead of straight ones, simply double-click a point so that two handles appear on either side. You have two choices from here.

If you drag the actual point, you can change the curvature of the line. Alternatively, you can move the side handles to make the line curve in two opposite directions (like a mirrored wave).

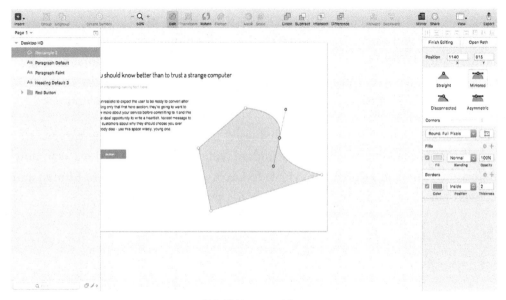

5-9. Making curved lines

Point Modes

By the way, that point is now called a **mirrored** point. If you observe the Inspector, you'll see that **Mirrored** is selected, whereas all the other points are **Straight**. Sketch has four point modes in total, two of which (**Straight** and **Mirrored**) can be toggled by double-clicking a point. **Disconnected** and **Asymmetric** are the other two, but they can only be selected using the Inspector interface. Let's summarize what they do:

---

[1] https://en.wikipedia.org/wiki/B%C3%A9zier_curve

- **Straight**: a straight line with zero control handles
- **Mirrored**: a curve with two symmetrical mirrored handles
- **Asymmetric**: a curve with two *asymmetric* mirrored handles
- **Disconnected**: both control handles are independent of each other

Point modes offer a huge deal of flexibility, letting us draw shapes non-destructively and independently of resolution. It can take some time to master the art of drawing vectors, so don't worry too much if you find this a little challenging at first.

Edit for Bitmaps

Does the **Edit** tool work on bitmaps? Yes, but since bitmaps are not drawn mathematically, **Edit** works a little differently in comparison to vectors. Bitmap images are made up of individual square *pixels*, and Sketch lets us do *no more* than select certain areas of a bitmap and apply either a crop or fill action.

As I've mentioned a few times, Sketch doesn't handle bitmap editing very well, and the tools available are extremely underdeveloped. If you're curious as to how **Selection**, **Crop** and **Fill** work, navigate to **Layer → Flatten Section to Bitmap** and convert our shape to a bitmap. Press **enter** to open the tools.

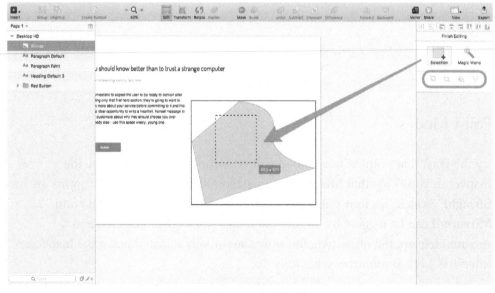

5-10. Selecting an area of the bitmap

Inserting and Replacing Bitmaps

We'll come back to vectors and explore something a little more complex shortly. For now, let's delete our wacky vector shape and insert an image into the canvas. Start by copying an image to the clipboard either from the internet, Photoshop, or some other bitmap editing tool. Paste it (**cmd + P**) into the canvas.

I'd suggest using Smart Guides here, so hold **option** to ensure the image is moved to a non-random location. In my example, I've included a trendy device mockup, and I think it looks quite suitable when surrounded by 70px of negative space.

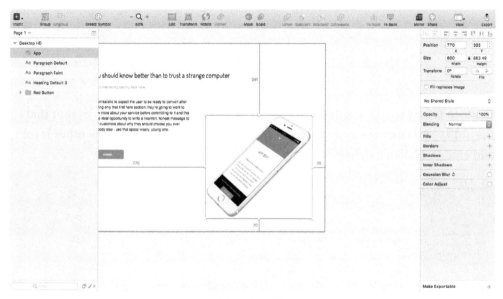

5-11. Inserting a bitmap

Replacing Bitmaps

It's not that Sketch's bitmap editing capabilities are in some way bad: Sketch simply wasn't built to accomplish such tasks. Sketch users are expected to create detailed artwork elsewhere, so when a bitmap in Sketch needs to be changed, we should edit it in something like Photoshop and use Sketch's **Replace Image…** feature, which can be accessed from the context menu. After clicking it, a file-selection dialog will appear.

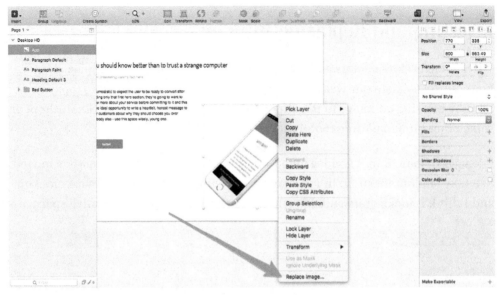

5-12. Replacing an updated image

Replace Image works similarly to the Layer List feature **Paste Over**, except that the old layer is deleted and replaced, whereas **Paste Over** retains the other layer and simply blocks its view.

5-13. Replaced

Masking

Our next adventure will involve the technique of "masking", so we'll be designing a big header with a bitmap background.

Masking is about using shapes (rectangles, stars, whatever) as a base, and making sure that overlapping layers don't leak outside this base. Anything that exceeds the boundary of the base (known as the "mask") is clipped off. Let's tackle an issue where a background image might exceed the boundaries of its container.

Press **A** and select the same Artboard as before—Desktop HD—and then draw a rectangle with the following styles:

- Width: 100%
- Height: 900px
- Fill: 04A777
- Border: **remove**

Snap this rectangle to the top left of the Artboard.

5-14. We're designing a header

Now we're going to need a large image to blend into this newly created rectangle (following the "big header" trend). When you've found something, use the **Paste Over** method (**context menu → Paste Over**) and apply the following styles:

- Width: 100%
- Opacity: 50%
- Blending: Soft Light
- Color Adjust → Saturation: 0

5-15. Blending an image into the background

As you can see, the blended image is a little larger than the rectangle, which is undesirable and very annoying. But there's a way to fix this. Right-click on the rectangle layer (from the Layer List, since it isn't directly clickable on the canvas anymore) to open up the context menu and choose **Use as Mask**.

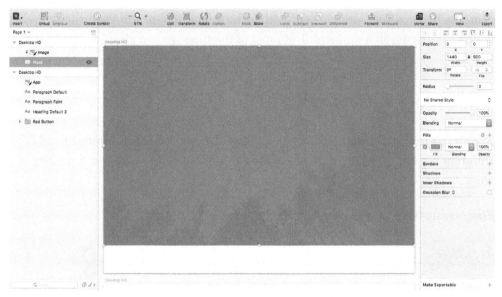

5-16. Masking layers

Not only is the image now being masked by the rectangle, but any future layers will be masked by this rectangle too, indicated with a down arrow next to the layer icon in the Layer List.

Breaking a Group out of a Mask

Should a future layer need to "break away" from the mask, you have two options: you can either group (**cmd + G**) all of the masked layers (including the mask itself)—effectively restricting the mask to only that group—or you can right-click a masked layer and select **Ignore Underlying Mask**.

Boolean Operations

So we have the basis of a "big header" section, and I think what it really needs now is a navigation icon—which brings us back to drawing vectors. Since vectors are one of the most complicated aspects of Sketch, I thought we'd take a little break, talk about masking, and then revisit vectors again.

This time around we'll discuss **boolean operations**, which involve adding **subpaths** to an existing path—or in simpler terms, combining shapes with other shapes to create more complex vectors. Sometimes the shape we need is so complex that we must draw it with either the **Pencil** tool or the **Vector** tool, which I'll discuss in a moment. But most of the time we can simply create shapes like rectangles and ovals and combine them using these boolean operations.

How Boolean Operations Work

Sketch has four different boolean operations—**Union**, **Subtract**, **Intersect** and **Difference**—and they all combine shapes in different ways. Let's see how they work.

First, create two circles and have them intersect one another.

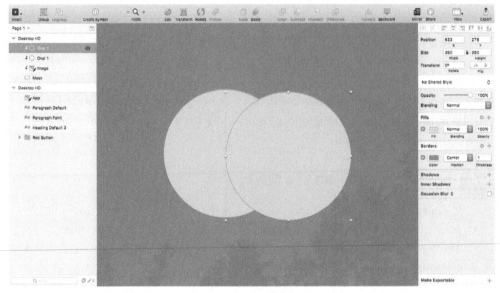

5-17. Intersected circles

Now select both circles at once and choose the **Union** operation from the toolbar. Right away you'll notice that these two circles have now become one shape. If you click the drop-down icon next to this vector shape (in the Layer List), you'll see that both of our original shapes still exist, because boolean operations are non-destructive. Our original shape has been renamed to "Path"; any other shapes in the vector are called subpaths. Styles for vector shapes are inherited from the path, not the subpaths.

5-18. Merging shapes

Select both circles again, but this time choose **Subtract**, and observe how the subpath is subtracted from the main path.

5-19. Subtract

Let's try **Intersect** now. What's left over from the boolean operation is the area where the two shapes overlap.

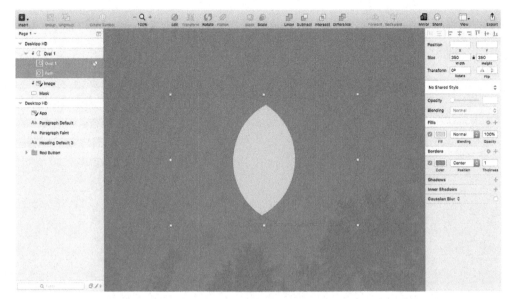

5-20. Intersect

Finally, **Difference**. Difference is the area where the two shapes don't overlap, so basically the opposite of **Intersect**.

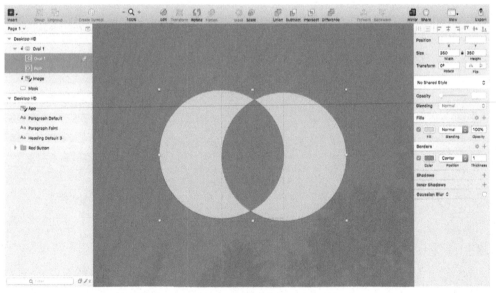

5-21. Difference

Using Boolean Operations to Create an Icon Design

Draw a rectangle with the following styles:

- Width: 300
- Height: 50
- Radius: 13
- Fill: FFFFFF
- Border: **remove**

Hold **option** while dragging the rectangle to duplicate it, then drop it 50px above the first rectangle. Repeat this step, select all of the rectangles, and choose **Union** to combine all of the paths into a single vector shape. Well done, you've designed your first vector icon—the trendy "hamburger" navigation icon.

5-22. Your first vector design

But we're not done yet. It's far too big!

Select the icon (make sure you're selecting the entire shape, and not one of the individual paths) and change the height to 24, using the Inspector. In order to maintain the aspect ratio, click the lock icon. You'll notice that the corners of the paths look a little more rounded than desired. That's because we've resized the icon but the corner radius is still 13px.

Press **cmd + Z** to undo your steps. Instead, use the **Scale** tool, which will not only resize the icon with the aspect ratio automatically maintained, but it will also scale all numerical, value-based styles such as shadows and corner radiuses too.

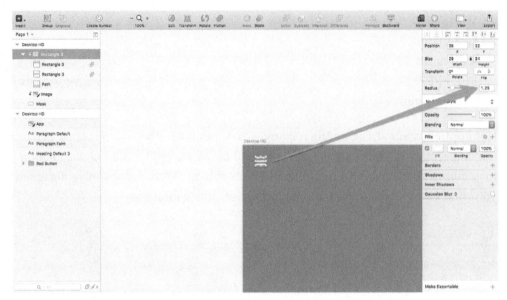

5-23. 13px is scaled to 1.25px

Vector Tool

You can also tap **V** on the keyboard to activate the **Vector** tool and create vectors from scratch. As with the **Pencil** tool (which I'll talk about shortly), drawing vectors requires a firm hand and an admirable commitment to illustration.

In most situations, you can sail smoothly by combining shapes—as we've been doing so far. But if you need to draw more custom shapes, **Vector** will be your savior.

Pencil Tool

Do vectors have to be geometric? *No.* If you tap **P** on the keyboard, you'll activate the **Pencil** tool, which will let you draw any organic shape you can think of. If you're a little shaky with a mouse, this may not be the best tool for you—although, as with all vectors, you can mold them into something much neater (with fewer vector points) afterwards. **Pencil** is useful for drawing *highly* *irregular* shapes, as opposed to combining rather standard shapes with boolean operations.

Normally, **Pencil** is used quite sparingly, as "hand-drawn" vectoring is better suited to an app like Illustrator, which has more refined vector drawing tools.

Summary

In this chapter, not only did we learn about the differences between bitmap and vector images, but we learned how to create, edit and use them too. More importantly, we're learning how to complete actions (both simple and complex) without the use of interfaces, allowing us to keep a keen eye on the canvas and iterate ideas in the quickest, easiest way imaginable.

In the following chapter, we'll explore Grid Settings and Layout Settings, and how applying these foundations to an Artboard before starting a design can help us regulate layouts that are more modular—as opposed to our current mockup, which offers a lot of negative space and flexibility.

Chapter

6

Rulers and Grids

Rulers and Grids help us to measure layers and distribute them steadily, which is an important step to take regardless of what you're actually designing. Many web designs are required to obey a strict layout for consistency, especially modular layouts and websites that will eventually be coded using a CSS framework such as Bootstrap or Foundation—and that's where Layout Grids come in handy. For icons and logos, Layout Grids wouldn't be suitable. Instead we'd use the much simpler Regular Grids.

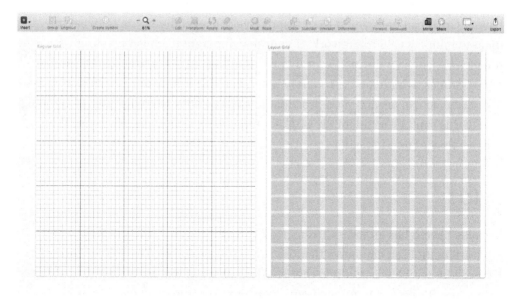

6-1. Regular Grids and Layout Grids

Let's define those right now.

What Are Regular Grids For?

Regular Grids consist of squares that are evenly distributed into rows and columns. If you're not familiar with Grids at all, rows are the squares that tile horizontally and columns are the squares that tile vertically, effectively forming a Grid.

With Regular Grids, all rows and columns are the same width and height, although each square will be further split into smaller squares, making them very useful for designing vector-based objects such as icons, logos and simple-ish illustrations.

What Are Layout Grids For?

Layout Grids are a little more sophisticated. When it comes to screens, not only do we need to account for the modules that make up our design, but also the spacing (known as the **gutter**) between those modules. It's not as simple as working with a Regular Grid of squares, although both are very easy to set up.

Layout Grids can help you design responsively, especially if you're tweaking them to mimic a CSS framework. If your development team isn't coding with a framework, you can normally survive without Layout Grids and instead rely on Smart Guides, which are only visible when you need them to be, resulting in a far less cluttered canvas and more freedom to explore alternative layouts. That being said, Grids can't be accidentally clicked or moved when interacting with the canvas: they're non-invasive.

Rulers

Because Sketch has an unlimited canvas, the Rulers aren't fixed to a specific, arbitrary point. You can move the Rulers (by dragging them) to define your own zero-origin, which is actually rather similar to how you'd use a ruler in real life. As always, it's easiest to understand a concept by doing it, so create a "Desktop HD" Artboard once more (we can do this in a totally new document), and then a create a rectangle of any random size.

Press **control + R** to toggle the Rulers on.

Drag the horizontal Ruler so that the zero-origin starts at the rectangle's left side, and then measure how wide the rectangle is. This will be indicated by the slightly grayed area that appears on the Ruler whenever you select a layer in the Artboard.

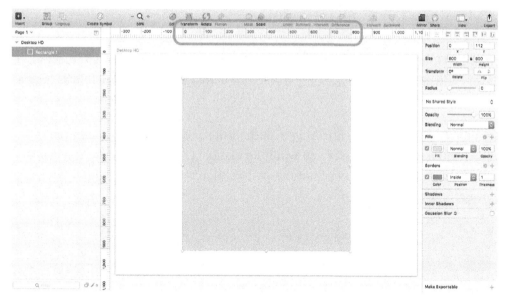

6-2. Moving the zero-origin

You can reset the zero-origin by clicking on the intersection between the horizontal and vertical Rulers, which (by default) aligns to the top left side of the currently selected Artboard.

6-3. Resetting the zero-origin

Setting Manual Guides

Manual Guides look exactly like Smart Guides, because their lines are red and layers will snap to them. The only difference is that they remain visible as long as Rulers are switched on.

Manual Guides are set by hovering over the Rulers (on either axis) and then clicking the Rulers wherever you want the manual Guides to appear. You can drag them outside the canvas (not the Artboard) to remove them (which is currently the only way).

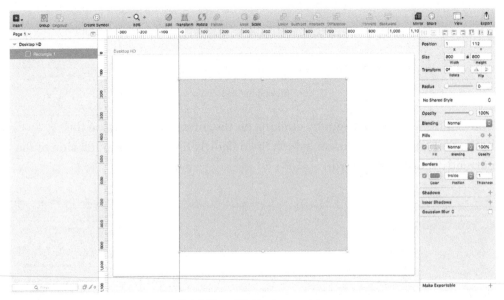

6-4. A Manual Guide at zero-origin

Manual Guides are useful if you need to quickly size something up, but they won't help you if you're trying to design to specification. For that, you'll need Regular and Layout Grids.

How to Specify Regular Grid Settings

As I mentioned before, Regular Grids are equally spaced, and that makes them excellent for creating icons and logos. Press **control + G** to turn them on, then try moving the rectangle shape around. You'll notice that the edges of the rectangle have begun snapping to the many squares in the Grid. Some of the squares are larger (as indicated by the thicker lines), and some of the squares are smaller (as indicated by the thinner lines).

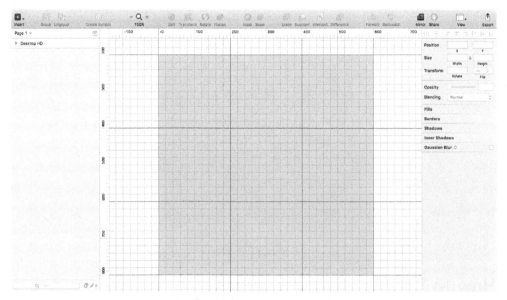

6-5. Regular Grids zoomed in at 100%

You can change the size of the squares and the regularity of thick lines by navigating to **View → Canvas → Grid Settings….** By default, the Grid size is 20px and the thick lines appear every 10 squares. You can change the default in the dialog window.

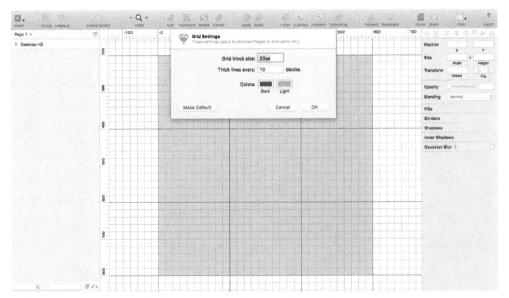

6-6. Regular Grid settings

How to Specify Layout Settings

Layout Grids are ideal for designing websites. Press **control + L** to turn them on and navigate to **View → Canvas → Layout Settings...** to see what options are available. Layout Grids are a little more complex in comparison to Regular Grids, but it's nothing we can't handle. Let's go through the settings.

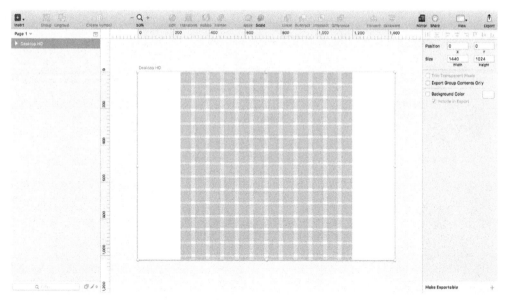

6-7. Layout Grids in action

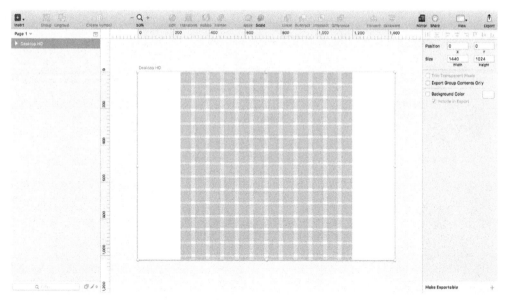 Total Width: the width of your main content

Offset: the offset distance from the zero-origin

Center: centers the Layout Grid in the Artboard

Gutter on outside: this relates to `box-sizing` in CSS

Gutter Width: the space between columns

Column Width: the width of individual columns

Gutter Height: the space between rows

Row Height: defined as a multiple of Gutter Height

Visuals: changes the visual look of the Layout Grid

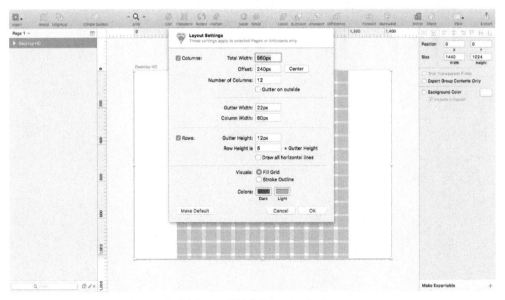

6-8. Layout Grids being customized

As you can see, Layout Grids can be customized down to the tiniest detail to suit either your unique layout, or the CSS framework you aim to use later on in the development stage.

Recreating the Bootstrap Grid with Layout Grids

Bootstrap[1] is arguably one of the biggest and most commonly used CSS frameworks. So, as a quick exercise, let's recreate our Layout Grid to reflect Bootstrap's version. Here are the settings you'll need to recreate the Bootstrap grid for desktop (>1170px) layouts:

- Total Width: 1170px
- Offset: center
- Gutter on outside: *checked*
- Gutter Width: 30px
- Column Width: 68px

---

1. http://getbootstrap.com/

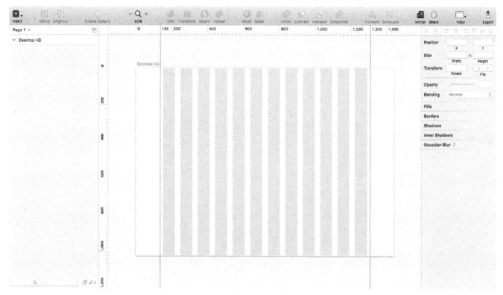

6-9. Bootstrap-optimized Layout Grids

Since the gutter is on the *outside*, I've included two manual Guides (using the Ruler) to illustrate where the Layout Grid actually starts and ends. The Total Width value—**1170px**—sets the distance between the first and second manual Guides.

 Making this Setup Default

If you use Bootstrap exclusively (or at least quite often), you might find it hugely beneficial to hit the **Make Default** button in the bottom left corner of the modal window—which will ensure that, by default, your Grids will be all set for Bootstrap layouts every time you start a new document.

Summary

In this chapter, we've discussed the various ways we can measure layers and design to specificity. It's not a terribly long chapter, mostly because Sketch makes designing a breeze.

In the next chapter, we'll discuss how Sketch users normally export image assets (both Retina and non-Retina) for websites, for apps, and for the app icons that accompany those apps. We'll also talk about local sharing, and how it can be used to share designs with your team as long as they're connected to the local network.

Chapter

7

Previewing Artboards and Exporting Assets

In this chapter, we'll take a look at two things: previewing designs on real devices, and exporting image assets when we're finally happy with them. Previewing can be done in two ways: either with Sketch Mirror, an iOS app that mirrors your Artboards to your devices, or with Local Sharing, which allows those in your team to view Artboards on their own desktops and devices—as long you're all connected to the same local network.

Previewing Artboards

Previewing designs is important, especially mobile designs. It's one of the many steps that make up user experience testing, and you can never really understand the user experience of your website or mobile app until you *become* the user. For mobile designs this means testing in a real device, but for desktop websites it means simply opening the designs in a browser.

Sketch Mirror

Sketch Mirror[1] is an iOS application that serves as a companion to Sketch. It casts your Artboards onto your iOS devices while you design, so that you can literally hold your device-optimized layout in a real device and see how it really looks.

 Previewing on Android

> Sadly, there's no (native) Android equivalent for this feature, though there is a tool called Skala Preview[2] that *can* send exported Artboards from your Mac to your Android devices. Instead of having to actually export Artboards, though, you can use the Sketch Preview Plugin instead, which sends Artboards directly to Android devices via Skala Preview.

Does your thumb comfortably reach all tappable elements on the screen? Are the main features of the website or app accessible with a minimal number of interactions? Does your above-the-fold content address the critical information? Previewing your designs prompts you to ask these vital questions—even if they aren't clickable, interactive or "working" prototypes.

Sketch Mirror is rather straightforward—both to set up and to use—but we'll do a quick and easy walkthrough anyway. You'll need to download it onto an iOS device first, costing around $4.99 from the App Store. When you're ready, open up Sketch Mirror on the device and it'll guide you through the setup.

---

1. https://itunes.apple.com/app/sketch-mirror/id677296955
2. https://bjango.com/help/skalapreview/sketch/

7-1. Sketch Mirror opening screen

The basic steps are:

1. connect your Mac and iOS device to the same Wi-Fi signal
2. open Sketch on the Mac
3. click on the "Mirror" toolbar icon
4. select your iOS device from the list

Since I'm creating these very screenshots with an iPad, I've created an iPad-optimized Artboard. If you're following along, feel free to recreate the design in whatever size Artboard you like, depending on what type of iOS device you have.

7-2. Starting up Sketch Mirror

After syncing the Mac and the iOS device, the first Artboard will show up on the device. Artboards can be navigated by swiping left or right. Pages can be navigated by swiping up or down.

Keep swiping left until you reach your mobile-optimized Artboard.

If you quickly tap on the device screen, a simple navigation with two menu items will appear at the bottom—Pages on the left, Artboards on the right. If you have a huge amount of screens in your document, using this navigation instead of swiping can really save you some time (and a sore thumb!).

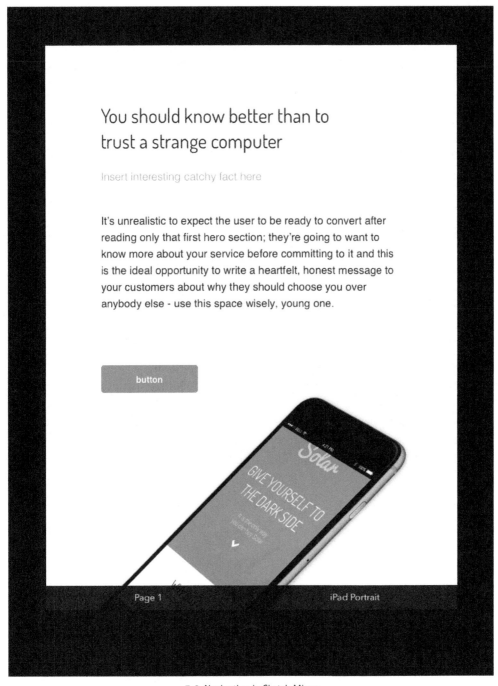

7-3. Navigating in Sketch Mirror

Try Connecting More Devices

Why not try connecting an additional Apple device and have them *both* update in real time as you continue designing?

Local Sharing

Local Sharing provides a means of sending your `.sketch` document to other team members without them ever needing a copy of Sketch themselves. Instead, they'll be able to preview the Artboards in their browser, and the only requirement is that they be connected to the same network as you—hence the term "local" sharing.

Sharing Artboards has many benefits:

- project managers can manage design tasks more easily
- developers can weigh in on the practicality of the design
- all team members can offer feedback without requiring Sketch
- remote teams can be assured that headway is being made
- the need for unnecessary and time-consuming meetings is reduced

Start by opening the `.sketch` design we've been building. In the toolbar (next to **Mirror**) you'll see an option called **Share**. Click it, and observe the modal dialog that appears. You'll see a switch button: click it to turn on Local Sharing.

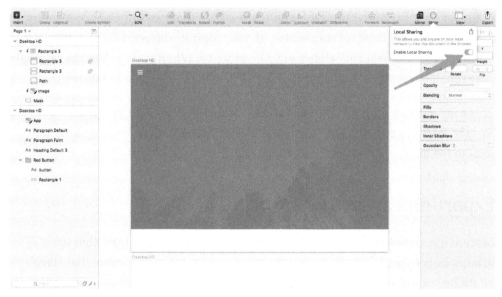

7-4. Local Network Sharing

Right away, the entire document will open in the browser, separated into Artboards, with the Artboard names visible—and you can click the Artboards to view them in full screen too.

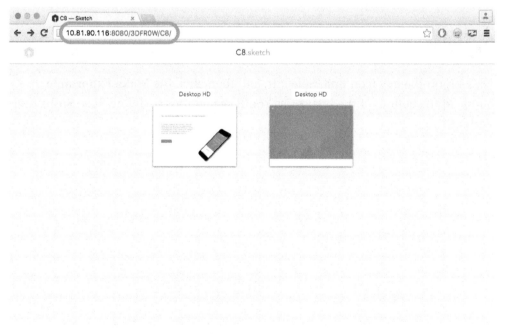

7-5. Previewing in the browser

In the address bar of the browser, you'll see a URL that can only be accessed by those on the same internet connection as you. Simply share this URL with your teammates to let them see what you've been up to. When you update the original .sketch document, each recipient of the URL will see the changes as well.

There are various plugins that extend the Artboard sharing functionality of Sketch. We'll discuss these in the next chapter, along with sharing options for remote teams.

Exporting Layers and Artboards

Since we're drawing towards the end of this book, it's only natural that we discuss how to move our image assets into the next stage. For some, that stage might be coding a website or app, and for others it might be a logo design that will eventually end up on some marketing materials. Either way, those image assets need to be exported so that we can use them further.

Exporting has always been a tiresome task in design, but Sketch handles it wonderfully by letting you automate the workflow. **Export** is arguably Sketch's most critically acclaimed feature.

Inspector

Let's export the nav icon first. Select it, and then click the **Make Exportable** button at the bottom of the Inspector. You'll see options to define **Size**, **Suffix** and **Format**.

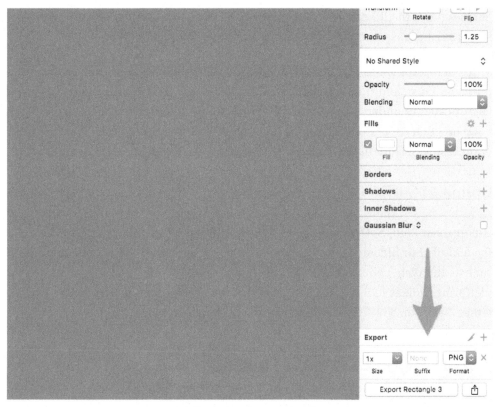

7-6. First look at the export interface

Option 1: Size

By "size" we mean **resolution**. If the size is set to "1x", the layer will be exported as displayed on the canvas at 100% zoom; "2x" will be double that size, and "3x" will be triple—suitable choices if you're supporting Retina/HiDPI devices.

 What is Retina?

> **Retina display** is technically a marketing term coined by Apple. It refers to devices (including desktop monitors) that have a higher-than-usual *pixel density*, also known as *ppi* or *pixels per inch*, which is usually around 300ppi or more.

With Retina-like devices, the display quality is noticeably higher because there are **more pixels per inch**. When Retina technology was first introduced to Apple devices (with the iPhone 4), we were required to export assets that were twice as large (2x), because the ppi for Retina devices was doubled to 326ppi.

Since then, Apple has managed to create devices with 401ppi (iPhone 6 and iPhone 6 Plus), and they ask that you export assets at "3x". It's a little complicated to understand at first, I'll admit. PaintCode has an excellent diagram[3] that accurately illustrates how the different iPhones scale Retina-optimized assets to display clear, crisp quality.

Option 2: Suffix

An optional field, **Suffix**, automatically appends characters of your choosing to the end of your filenames. Because Retina images are optional for some mediums, such as the Web, you can sometimes leave the suffix blank. However, as some platforms such as iOS require Retina-optimized images, it's customary to add either "@2x" or "@3x" to the filenames. Here's an example:

- **icon.png**: non-Retina images don't require a suffix
- **icon@2x.png**: for Retina devices that require 2x images
- **icon@3x.png**: for Retina devices that require 3x images

iOS devices will automatically choose the correct image, as detected by the suffix. If you need an arbitrary size that Sketch doesn't offer in the drop-down box, like "1.5x" for example, simply type it. Sketch can export to any size of your choosing.

 Include a Folder Name in the Export

If you rename the export in the Layer List beforehand to include a folder name, for example "folder/image", Sketch will export to that folder and even create it if it doesn't already exist. Folder names are relative to wherever you've chosen to export to.

Option 3: Format

Sketch supports a variety of formats:

[3.] http://www.paintcodeapp.com/news/ultimate-guide-to-iphone-resolutions

- JPG: for compressing images with no transparency
- PNG: for images with transparent areas (default option)
- TIFF: for high-quality images (also supports transparency)
- PDF/EPS: maintains vector qualities for use in Adobe apps
- SVG: a vector format for the Web, which can also be used in Adobe apps

PDF Assets for iOS

PDF assets are also often used in production iOS apps. It's a nice way to support 1x, 2x and 3x devices with a single asset.

Exporting Multiple Versions

We can export the same layer numerous times, optionally setting a different resolution, suffix and/or file format each time. Just click the + icon in the interface to add another row of options. By default, the new row will assume the variables of a 2x export and already have "@2x" in the suffix field.

You can have as many export combinations as you like, and even define your own resolutions in the **Size** field.

7-7. Exporting multiple versions

Removing the Export Option

You can click the **x** icon to remove that export option or click all of the **x** icons to make the layer no longer exportable.

Actually Exporting Layers

You don't have to export layers as they come. The exporting process can be automated with a keyboard shortcut (which we'll discuss shortly) at the end of the design stage, to export everything that's been made "exportable". Alternatively, you can click the **Export** button in the Inspector to export that specific layer right there and then.

For now, let's *not* export the icon, and move on to the app mockup image from the other Artboard. Don't worry, the export options for the icon layer will remain active; we'll come back to it.

Before we leave the icon layer though, rename it (**cmd + R**) to "images/nav-icon". After that, move on to the app mockup image and rename that layer to "images/ app-mockup". Now we have a dedicated folder for our image exports. Click **Make Exportable**, and—as with the icon layer—leave the settings at their default.

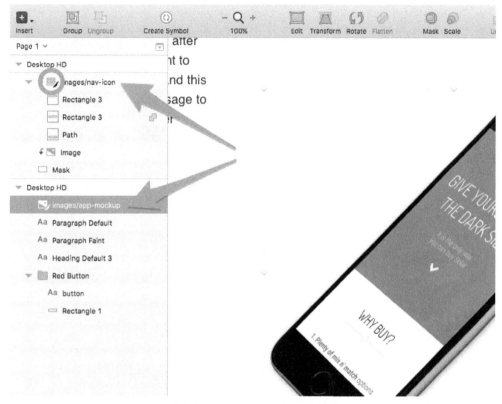

7-8. Both are renamed and exportable

Layers or groups that have been made exportable are indicated by a tiny knife icon in the Layer List. Should you ever encounter a situation where you can't remember if a layer is included in an export, check the icon next to it in the Layer List to find out.

You can use the keyboard shortcut **cmd + shift + E** to export (or re-export) all of your assets at once. A modal will appear asking you to confirm which assets you'd like to include in the export. Should any of the assets change in any way, you can run the command to begin automating the export operation once again.

7-9. Exporting all assets at once

 Quick Exports

You can drag layers from the Layer List to the desktop (or any other folder) for a "quick export" action. If you use Sketch in a maximized window, drag layers to the edges of the screen and wait a short moment until the screen slides over to the next. Quick exports come in PNG format and the resolution will be 1x.

Exporting Artboards

As an alternative to local sharing, some teams use design prototyping and user flow apps like InVision[4] and Marvel[5] because they have team collaboration tools built in. In this case, it's customary to export entire Artboards.

Prototyping apps are all the rage right now, and rightfully so, because they really do aid communication in teams and help to illustrate how one screen flows into another. It takes time to learn these apps—sort of how we're learning Sketch right now.

---

[4] http://www.invisionapp.com/sketch-prototyping

[5] https://marvelapp.com/

After selecting an Artboard, revert your eyes back to the Inspector. You may have noticed at some stage that there's an option called **Background Color**. Right now, our Artboard doesn't have a background: it *appears* to be white, but is actually transparent.

At the bottom of the Inspector, click **Make Exportable**. As you can see, the export preview shows that the background is transparent, indicated by a faint checkerboard background.

7-10. Previewing the transparent areas

In order to fix this, check the **Background Color** option and ensure that it's white. Immediately, the export preview will reflect this update. It's important to confirm that the sub-option, called **Include in Export**, is also checked.

7-11. Include background color in export

Exporting Slices

Slices are custom-defined areas of the canvas that can be exported to a single file. They can be drawn out like rectangles, or drawn *around* a layer. Either way, they appear like layers in the Layer List, and are inserted as such too (with the keyboard shortcut **S**). If you want to slice an area around a layer, use the **S** shortcut and then select that layer. Otherwise, draw a rectangle over the area you want to export to slice it.

You should imagine each individual Slice like custom-sized camera frame focused on a specific rectangular area—for example, a modal dialog (without the modal background). Slicing defines the area that you want to crop, and then you can quickly export it.

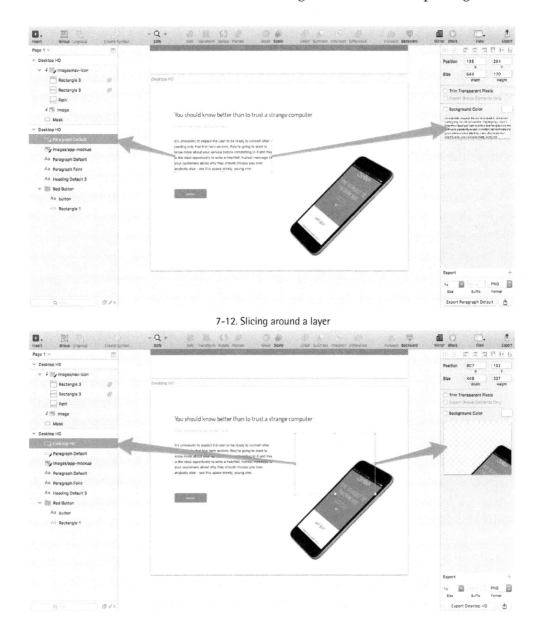

7-12. Slicing around a layer

7-13. Slicing a custom-defined region

Slices are *independent of other layers*. No matter what may change on the canvas behind the Slice—even if it was originally modeled around a specific layer—it won't move or change size, unless you move or resize it yourself. Slices have two settings to watch out for, both of which can be set via the inspector: Trim Transparent Pixels, and Export Group Contents Only.

Trim Transparent Pixels

Should the edges of the sliced area contain any transparent sections, the **Trim Transparent Pixels** option will shave them off. Since the aim of slicing is to crop a specific area from the Artboard, it's only natural that we'd want to keep the crop as small as we can. As always, the export preview appears in the Inspector, so observe the result when this option is checked:

7-14. Shaving off transparent areas

Export Group Contents Only

Because sliced areas are always rectangular, you may sometimes experience other layers creeping into the frame. The solution is to group the sliced area and the layers, and then check the **Export Group Contents Only** option, ensuring that the Slice only affects the layers you want it to work on.

Summary

In this chapter, we learned how to preview Artboards in the browser and real devices, and how to export the assets for further use in coding environments or elsewhere when finally happy with the results.

In the following chapter, we'll discuss plugins. Plugins are like add-ons to Sketch, or "extensions" if that term is more familiar to you. You can install them with minimal effort to add extra functionality and shortcuts (that Sketch doesn't have natively), reducing the time it takes to accomplish a task.

Chapter **8**

Plugins

Plugins are add-ons that extend the capabilities of Sketch far beyond what's natively available. Some of these slightly improve the user experience of repetitive tasks, and others integrate with external services such as Slack (for sharing designs with your team) and various prototyping apps such as Zeplin, Marvel, Framer and so on. Essentially, they make you more *productive* by allowing you to create a customized workflow that suits *you*.

Most of them come with a handy set of keyboard shortcuts. However, a recent change to Sketch's API has allowed developers to add graphical user interfaces (GUIs) to their plugins, raising hopes that we'll see more such developments in future.

Plugins can help you do such things as:

- source dummy text and images
- analyze and replace colors
- rename multiple layers on the fly
- duplicate app icons in various sizes
- add notes and annotations to Artboards
- create URLs for Artboards so you can share them

How to Install Plugins

Plugins can be installed in three ways: by downloading them into Sketch's **Plugins** folder, by opening a compressed .sketchplugin file, or via the Sketch Toolbox application.

1. Manual Installation

Let's start with the first method—the manual approach. Navigate to **Plugins** → **Manage Plugins**, click the cog icon, and then select **Show Plugins Folder**, which will open an actual folder from your Mac. Downloading plugins from the internet (usually GitHub) into this folder installs them.

2. Sketch Plugin Files

Plugin files can be compressed into a single file, which is actually an ordinary folder with the .sketchplugin extension. You only need to open the file (double-click, for example) and it will self install.

Self-installing formats make life much easier than having to locate the Plugins folder and copy files into it. However, there's a third option that not only makes it delightfully straightforward to *find and install* plugins, but also to *remove* them. It's a Mac application called Sketch Toolbox.

3. Sketch Toolbox

Sketch Toolbox[1] is a free, independent Mac application created by Shahruz Shaukat. It lets you search for and install plugins without having to locate the folder. It also helps you tool up your workflow within seconds.

Start by installing the app and opening it.

8-1. Sketch Toolbox

You'll see two tabs in the top left corner—one for plugins that you can download (**All**), and another for plugins that you already have (**Installed**). Besides that, there's a **check for updates** icon, which is useful because most plugins are hosted on GitHub. (It's otherwise quite time-consuming to update them manually.)

When something interesting catches your eye, click the **Install** button—but remember: only ever install plugins that are regularly updated, because future versions of Sketch may break them; too many may also result in conflicting keyboard shortcuts.

All in all, I would recommend using Sketch Toolbox over other methods due to its simplicity and variation. However, it's important to remember that Sketch

---

1. http://sketchtoolbox.com/

Toolbox doesn't house every single plugin there is. You should start with Sketch Toolbox, but diversify your search with Google, Sketch App Sources[2], or Sketch's own curated list[3] if you can't find the type of functionality you need.

Useful Sketch Plugins

Let's walk through some of the most useful extensions.

Clipboard Fill

Sketch actually supports a background image fill for shapes, but it's a bit of a hack. If you select **Fill** → **Pattern Fill** → **Fill (dropdown)** from the Inspector and then choose an image to upload, it will use the image as a background as if you were using the shape as a mask. However, you can't edit this image, since it isn't technically a separate layer.

Clipboard Fill[4] takes an image that you've copied to the clipboard and inserts it into a shape as a background fill, eliminating the need to delve into the actual **Fill** interface. Shall we try it out? Create three circles (**O** is the keyboard shortcut you need here) and multiple-select them (click while holding **shift**), like so:

[2.] http://www.sketchappsources.com/plugins-for-sketch.html

[3.] http://www.sketchapp.com/extensions/plugins/

[4.] https://github.com/scottsavarie/clipboard-fill

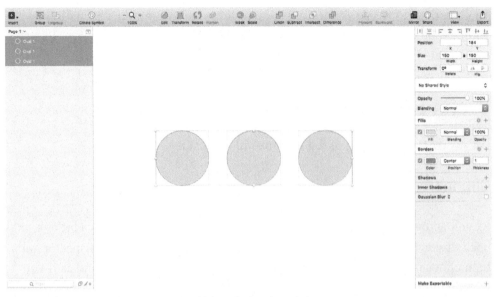

8-2. Make and select three circles

Press **control + option + V** and see the magic unfold.

8-3. Multiple fill backgrounds

Replace Color

At the time of writing, Sketch doesn't offer a way to replace recurring colors (even if you're saving them using **Document Colors**), so this add-on is extremely useful, especially if you're always being asked to "make all the colors *pop*".

Sketch Replace Colour[5] detects what color-based styles (fill, border, text color) you're using on a layer and offers to replace them *document-wide*. Press **control + shift + R** after selecting a layer to open a the dialog box and begin the replacement.

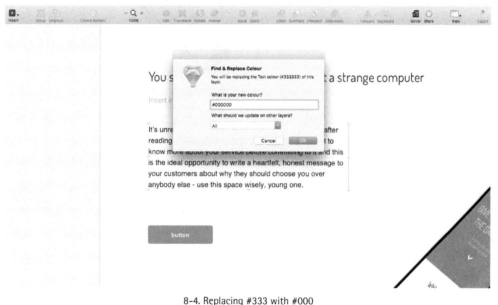

8-4. Replacing #333 with #000

Share Artboards with Easy Share

We've already discussed Local Sharing, but if you work remotely it won't help you in the slightest, because it requires your team to be connected via a local network. Easy Share[6] takes a snapshot of your Artboard and creates a self-expiring link to it, which you can then send to your team via email, messenger, or even Slack.

[5.] https://github.com/lewishowles/sketch-replace-colour
[6.] https://github.com/ed-lea/easyshare.sketchplugin

Select your Artboard (*not* any of the layers *in* the Artboard) and hit the keyboard shortcut **cmd + option + E**.

8-5. Firstly, select the Artboard

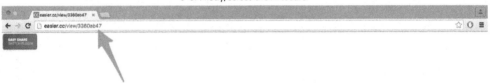

You should know better than to trust a strange computer

Insert interesting catchy fact here

It's unrealistic to expect the user to be ready to convert after reading only that first hero section; they're going to want to know more about your service before committing to it and this is the ideal opportunity to write a heartfelt, honest message to your customers about why they should choose you over anybody else - use this space wisely, young one.

8-6. Secondly, visit the link

Send Artboards to Slack

Slack[7] is a much admired team communication app that allows integrations with other collaboration apps. With the use of the Send to Slack[8] plugin, we can send Artboards to our Slack rooms to open up the conversation to design feedback and discussion.

Setting up this custom integration is quite easy:

1. go to the token generator[9]
2. find your Slack team in the list and click **Create token**
3. highlight and copy the token to the clipboard
4. go to **Plugins → Sketch To Slack → Update API Token** in Sketch
5. paste the token into the field and click **Ok**
6. navigate back to **Plugins → Sketch To Slack**
7. select a channel or user to send Artboards to

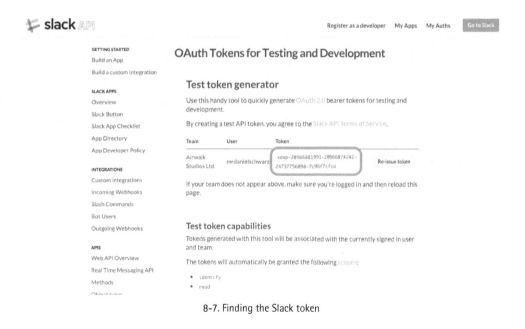

8-7. Finding the Slack token

---

7. https://slack.com
8. https://github.com/shahruz/Send-to-Slack
9. https://api.slack.com/docs/oauth-test-tokens

Style Layers with CSS

CSS Buddy[10] opens a dialog window that accepts CSS code—ideal for those designer/developer types that find it easier to type code rather than navigate interfaces. Just select the layer you need to style, use the keyboard shortcut **cmd + shift + A** and write some code.

8-8. Write code, click **Continue**

Automatically Source Placeholder Data

InVision recently released Craft[11], which is designed to source and insert placeholder data into Sketch. Even before its release, there were many "dummy data" plugins around—which you can browse through using Sketch Toolbox to see if something fits you better. However, Craft takes care of all kinds of dummy data in a single extension.

Let's start by inserting a random image from Unsplash[12] (a free photo sharing site). You can insert images from the Web, from a folder on your computer, or

---

10. https://github.com/jodyheavener/CSS-Buddy
11. http://labs.invisionapp.com/craft
12. https://unsplash.com/

even from your Dropbox account. Unsplash is useful for sourcing a completely random image if you don't have one already.

So, create a shape layer, select the **Photos** tab (Craft has an interface hanging off the side of the Inspector), choose **Unsplash**, and then click on the **Place Photo** button.

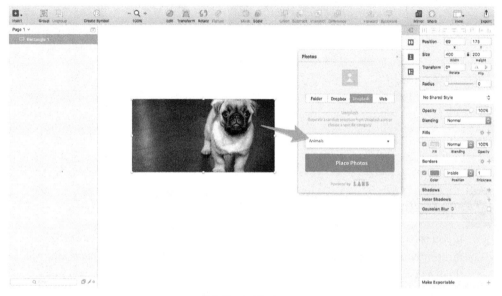

8-9. Placeholder images

Alternatively, you can select the **Type** tab and let Craft come up with random article titles, fake names, dummy article content and so on. All you need is a layer for Craft to insert the data *into*. You may have noticed three blank boxes at the bottom of the interface: if you select the edit icon, you can add more fields to this interface or remove fields that you don't need.

8-10. Dummy text

 Extracting data

If you select **Web** from the **Photos** or **Type** tabs, you'll be able to navigate within a mini-browser and extract data from the Web. You can even extract images and use them as backgrounds on text layers. Hold **cmd** when you click to navigate links.

Craft feels quite impressive for a first version—more like a lavish toolset than a simple extension. Aside from being able to insert "real data" in a variety of ways, it also offers a feature that lets you duplicate content both horizontally and vertically while requesting new dummy data for each duplicate.

If you select one or more layers and then the **Duplicate** tab, you can tile entire components in any direction. Craft will also organize the duplicates into groups—even if you haven't already!

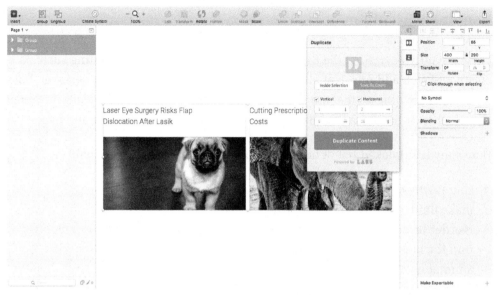

8-11. Duplicating dummy data

Collaborative Plugins

Many designers choose to integrate Sketch with their favorite collaborative tools in an effort to maintain effective communications with their team, and of course to receive feedback and prototype interactions or user flows as well. Since these are very workflow specific, I'd encourage you to look into each integration's official documentation for setup instructions:

- Sketch to GitHub[13]
- Sketch to Slack[14]
- Sketch to Framer[15]
- Sketch to Marvel[16]
- Sketch to Zeplin[17]
- Sketch to Origami[18]

---

[13] https://git.io/vg59N
[14] https://git.io/vgdcf
[15] https://git.io/vgdnR
[16] https://git.io/vgdRB
[17] https://git.io/vgdzT
[18] https://git.io/vgdRD

Honorable Mentions

I'm constantly amazed at the Sketch developer community for building such creative Sketch add-ons. Not all of them fit the needs of the average designer, but there are some plugins that are simply too awesome to not mention, and they may come in handy for those who have to repeat very specific tasks over and over.

Here's my handpicked list of honorable mentions for added functionality:

- share Artboards via QR code[19]
- make fluid, constraints-based Artboards[20]
- reorder layers[21]
- find the most common color in an image[22]
- annotate Artboards with sidebar notes[23]
- mass-rename layers[24]
- mass-duplicate Artboards into icon sizes[25]
- preview Artboards on any device[26]

Building Your Own Plugins

Plugins wouldn't exist without the Sketch Developer Community[27], a dedicated resource for Sketch users that helps them build their own extensions. You'll need to be able to code with CocoaScript (JavaScript and Cocoa), but the developer documentation does offer code examples, reference sheets and a ton of resources to help you learn more about it.

[19.] https://git.io/vgdkP
[20.] https://git.io/vgdtr
[21.] https://git.io/vgds0
[22.] https://git.io/vgdJ7
[23.] https://git.io/vgdaX
[24.] https://git.io/vgdwq
[25.] https://git.io/vgdab
[26.] https://git.io/v2xc4
[27.] http://developer.sketchapp.com/

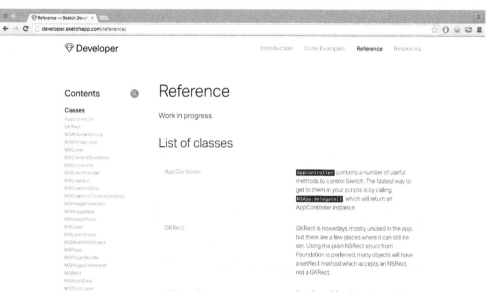

8-12. API reference sheet for developers

Summary

Plugins can offer an exceptional amount of value to a design workflow. In this final chapter, we've learned about the various ways we can find and install them, and we've also explored how some of them work as well. But don't stop there. Open up the Sketch Toolbox and start exploring new workflows!

Afterword

Now that you know how to use Sketch, it's time to try out some of the awesome collaborative tools that integrate with it, and also download some useful .sketch resources. I mention many of the best blogs, tools, resources and marketplaces in the Appendix, along with a concise list of keyboard shortcuts for Sketch.

One resource, the Solar UI Kit, is available in my Creative Market shop[28]. During the course of this book, I described how to recreate two sections of this user interface kit, so if you enjoyed working with it, feel free to take a look at the full .sketch file on Creative Market.

[28.] https://creativemarket.com/mrdanielschwarz

As for collaboration tools, it does take a small amount of time to learn how to use them. But if you've enjoyed using Sketch, I'd encourage you (and your team!) to explore a few of them.

InVision (the company behind the Craft prototyping tool) recently acquired Silver Flows[29], an extension designed to facilitate prototyping and user flows *directly* in Sketch. Now that InVision has acquired Silver Flows, it will become an integral feature of the Craft plugin, which is another reason I'd recommend starting with Craft.

And finally, I'd like to thank you for reading my book. I sincerely hope that the information, tutorials, tools and resources discussed in this book have brought you a huge step closer to being the user interface designer you'd like to be—one that can design with confidence and excellence in Sketch, the app that so many have come to love in recent years.

[29.] http://silverflows.com/

Appendix A: Keyboard Shortcuts and Useful Resources

Sketch's approach to keyboard shortcuts is revolutionary for a desktop graphic application. Adobe apps are well known for their bloated (and seemingly impossible) keyboard shortcuts, but Bohemian Coding's decision to keep Sketch focused only on vector and user interface design has resulted in fewer tools, and therefore easier shortcuts—some of which consist of a single keystroke.

 Handy Keyboard Stickers

If you have trouble remembering shortcuts, SketchKeys[1] can help you out; it's a set of keyboard stickers covering the main Sketch shortcuts.

Insert

You can insert objects by clicking **Insert** in the toolbar, but it's quicker to use these single-keystroke shortcuts:

- Artboard: **A**
- Rectangle: **R**
- Rounded Rectangle: **U** (rectangle with 8px radius)
- Oval: **O**
- Line: **L**
- Vector: **V**
- Pencil: **P**
- Text: **T**
- Slice: **S**

Type

- Bold: **cmd + B**
- Italic: **cmd + I**

[1.] http://sketchkeys.com/

- Underline: **cmd + U**
- Increase Font Size: **cmd + option + plus sign**
- Decrease Font Size: **cmd + option + minus sign**
- Increase Character Spacing: **control + option + L**
- Decrease Character Spacing: **control + option + T**
- Change Font: **cmd + T**
- Align Left: **cmd + shift + {**
- Align Center: **cmd + shift + |**
- Align Right: **cmd + shift + }**
- Special Characters: **cmd + control + space**
- Convert Text to Outlines: **cmd + shift + O** (i.e. to *paths*)

Canvas

- Zoom In: **cmd + plus sign**
- Zoom Out: **cmd + minus sign**
- Actual Size: **cmd + 0**
- Center Canvas: **cmd + 1**
- Zoom Selection: **cmd + 2**
- Center Selection: **cmd + 3**
- Temporary Zoom to Actual Size: **§** or **shift + ~**
- Focus on First Input Field (inspector): **option + tab**
- Toggle Rulers: **control + R**
- Toggle Grid: **control + G**
- Toggle Layout Guides: **control + L**
- Toggle Pixels: **control + P**
- Toggle Selection Handles: **control + H**
- Toggle Pixel Grid: **control + X** (when zoomed-in >800%)
- Move Canvas: **space + drag** (for those without a trackpad)

Window

- Toggle Between Documents: **cmd + ~** (on supported keyboards)
- Toggle Layer List: **cmd + option + 1**
- Toggle Inspector: **cmd + option + 2**
- Toggle Layer List and Inspector: **cmd + option + 3**

Toggle Toolbar: **cmd + T**
Presentation Mode: **cmd + .**
Fullscreen Mode: **cmd + control + F**

Editing Shapes

Keep Current Selection: **cmd + option**
Use as Mask: **cmd + control + M**
Resize Object: **cmd + arrows**
Resize Object (10px increments): **cmd + shift + arrows**
Union: **cmd + option + U**
Subtract: **cmd + option + S**
Intersect: **cmd + option + I**
Difference: **cmd + option + X**
Change Vector Point Style: **1**, **2**, **3** or **4**

Editing Layers

Show Smart Guides: **option**
Click-Through to Group: **cmd + click**
Smart Guides + Click-Through: **cmd + option**
Duplicate: **cmd + D** or **option + drag**
Copy Style: **cmd + option + C**
Paste Style: **cmd + option + V**
Color Picker: **control + C**
Transform: **cmd + T**
Rotate: **cmd + shift + R**
Toggle Fill: **F**
Toggle Border: **B**

Arranging Artboards, Groups and Layers

Bring Forward: **cmd + option + ↑**
Send Backward: **cmd + option + ↓**
Bring to Front: **cmd + option + control + ↑**

- Send to Back: **cmd + option + control + ↓**
- Hide: **cmd + shift + H**
- Lock: **cmd + shift + L**
- Rename: **cmd + R**
- Group Layers: **cmd + G**
- Ungroup Layers: **cmd + shift + G**
- Select Layer Above: **shift + tab**
- Select Layer Below: **tab**
- Select Parent Artboard: **esc**
- Find Layer by Name: **cmd + F**
- Select Page Above: **fn + ↑**
- Select Page Below: **fn + ↓**

Sketch Resources

- Sketch Land[2]
- Sketch Repo[3]
- Sketch Hunt[4]
- Sketch Tricks[5]
- Freebies Bug[6]
- Sketch App Sources[7]
- Sketch Facebook Group[8]
- Sketch App TV[9]

Marketplaces That Sell Sketch Files

- UI8[10]

---

[2] http://sketch.land/
[3] https://sketchrepo.com/
[4] http://sketchhunt.com/
[5] http://sketchtricks.com/
[6] http://freebiesbug.com/sketch-freebies/
[7] http://www.sketchappsources.com/
[8] https://www.facebook.com/groups/sketchformac/
[9] http://sketchapp.tv/
[10] https://ui8.net/category/sketch

- Creative Market[11]
- DesignModo[12]
- Visual Hierarchy[13]

Collaboration Tools That Support Sketch

- InVision App[14]
- Flinto[15]
- Marvel App[16]
- Proto.io[17]
- Zeplin[18]

---

[11] https://creativemarket.com/apps/sketch

[12] http://market.designmodo.com/

[13] https://visualhierarchy.co/shop/

[14] http://www.invisionapp.com/

[15] https://www.flinto.com/

[16] https://marvelapp.com/

[17] https://proto.io/

[18] https://zeplin.io/

CPSIA information can be obtained
at www.ICGtesting.com
Printed in the USA
BVOW10s0903060516

447063BV00005B/45/P